THE ART OF
LEARNING

The Art of Learning

.

Acknowledgments

A number of individuals contributed to the idea behind this book.

This includes:
Minister Mr Heng Swee Keat, Minister for Education, Singapore.
Professor Tan Chorh Chuan, President of National University of Singapore.
Professor Richard Brodhead, President of Duke University.
Professor Victor Dzau, President of Institute of Medicine, National Academies, USA.
Professor Tan Eng Chye, Deputy President (Academic Affairs) Provost of National University of Singapore.
Dr William Haseltine, Chairman of Access Health.
In particular, the book was shaped by the valuable comments and insights from Professor Robert Kamei and Associate Prof Sandy Cook at Duke–NUS.

The edits by Nils Parker from Command+Z Content took an unfinished version and turned it to a more readable tome. Wee Lai Ming assisted in moving the project along and helping to ensure that the project was a success.

This book would not have been possible without the indulgent support and tolerance of my wife Sripriya and my children, Vaishnavi and Prahlad.

The Art of Learning: Learn to Learn:

This book teaches the key principles that will help improve learning for everyone: children, students, adults, and in fact anyone that has to learn any subject, anytime and anywhere.

The techniques and rules described in this book are derived from the fundamental science of how we learn. It is easy to read and quickly shows the path to learning by using a set of simple, pragmatic rules; rules to build motivation and rules to speed up the learning process over both the short and the long term. As you read the book and begin this journey, you will enter a world of motivation, confidence, organization, memory, and learning. You will appreciate the rules, which are derived from our basic understanding of how the brain works during the learning process, and you will understand why these sometimes counterintuitive principles work so well.

By the time you reach the final chapter of the book, you will know how to apply these rules to your own learning. Use it is a map to help you navigate the world of learning and explore the enormous opportunities ahead.

The Art of Learning

Table of Contents

Foreword

It is with delight that I offer this foreword to Professor Ranga Krishnan's new book on learning, aptly titled 'The Art of Learning'. Professor Krishnan's first book on learning, *How to Lead*, which brought together the insightful series of essays first published in the Today newspaper, had drawn strong and enthusiastic responses, prompting him to put together this second book.

The Art of Learning presents the next steps for readers who want to build on the ideas and information in *How to Lead*, and move forward towards developing the skill sets and practices needed to become active and effective learners. The book offers a step-by-step instruction manual that bridges the connection between the latest research and the practical acquisition of skills. Professor Krishnan explains, clearly and accessibly, the key scientific understanding behind core topics related to learning, such as motivation, memory, repetition and practice, before outlining the exercises that will help you improve and integrate these powerful new learning skills.

As Professor Krishnan states early in the book, there is still much that we have to uncover about how humans acquire, and re-learn, new skills and knowledge. Nevertheless, what we have established so far already offers the possibility to transform human ability and potential. Professor Krishnan speaks not only from his expertise in psychiatry, but his experience as an inspired educator and innovator who has designed, led and fundamentally re-shaped medical education through Duke-NUS' paradigm-shifting teaching framework,

The Art of Learning

Team-LEAD (Learn, Engage, Apply and Develop). Team LEAD, which emphasises collaborative learning and closely ties principles and application in a dynamic environment, has turned out to be a game-changer that has drawn both local and global recognition and interest.

As Professor Krishnan observed, "Learning is natural" – it is an activity deeply embedded in human consciousness, and vital to our survival and adaptability. It is also an activity that can be enhanced with proper understanding and practices, leading to better learning outcomes, and expanded possibilities for continual self-development.

The Art of Learning is a unique text that blends fascinating science with practical implementation, and I hope readers will find Professor Krishnan's work both inspiring and highly applicable.

Professor Tan Chorh Chuan
President
National University of Singapore

Preface

Why this book and why now?

The word "learning" immediately brings to mind school, colleges, examinations and, lots of reading material. This book is about that and more.

Learning used to be defined by psychologists as a change in behaviour that occurs as a result of experience. But changes in behaviour are not an essential outcome for learning (although it might be a desired result) nor is it true to argue that a behaviour change was just due to learning. Changes in behaviour can happen because one is tired, sick, or bored and that is hard to attribute to just learning. And one can acquire knowledge without a change in observable behaviour—knowledge does not always lead to change. The knowledge that smoking is bad for our health does not necessarily lead to quitting cigarettes. Awareness or knowledge is not the same as a change in behaviour. Therefore, a more suitable definition for learning is, "the act of acquiring new knowledge, or altering and strengthening, existing knowledge skills and behaviour."

Learning is natural. It is something we are wired for and we learn from the time we are born. Learning is more than what we pick up in school; it constructs upon and is moulded by what we already know. More than that, learning is what makes us who we are as it shapes our habits, behaviours and choices. Given the impact and influence of learning, it is somewhat astonishing that more attention hasn't been given to it.

When it comes to learning there is much that we do not know. We are indeed at the very beginning of our journey to slowly unravel the mystery of learning. The shroud is slowly being lifted by work that has come to us from a variety of sources, fundamental research on everything from a sea slug, to insects, small mammals and of course humans.

There are many mysteries. Who can say what fires up a person to become a poet, tennis player, or doctor? Who can say why some of us can learn mathematics easily and others can learn to play professional sports with flair? We do not know the answers to why we do this and not that, but we have many clues as to how we get motivated and learn. It is indeed striking that many of us who are faculty are also unaware of the research in this arena.

Paradigm shifts in education will not be quick and instantaneous; they are more likely to be slow, prolonged and difficult. The word "paradigm" means a frame of reference, a model that can serve as a guide. Our commonly held mental models of how we learn seem intuitively right even though they are quite wrong. Many of our school systems, classrooms, and even our universities have fallen into this trap and have had difficulty breaking out of that mind-set. If you have the wrong model then whatever you do with that model will not get you far. Change is necessary.

I started at Duke 30 years ago as a faculty member in the Department of Psychiatry and Behavioural Medicine. Over these many years I have worked with scores of some of the brightest medical students, resident physicians and psychologists. It is surprising and indeed remarkable that during this period it was extremely rare to have a discussion on how we learn. We just followed time-honoured traditions of teaching lectures, discussions and the like without giving much thought to the processes behind them. We never questioned whether the paradigm that we all participated in worked. We just assumed that it did. Why else would it exist?

What was striking was that many of us worked on the scientific basis of emotion, working memory, and thinking without connecting what we did in our research to actually helping our students learn. In fact the connection between our research and the process of learning was right in front of us, but we never recognized the obvious.

About 15 years ago, I had the pleasure of starting to work with a passionate training director, Grace Thrall, who introduced what at that time seemed radically innovative: she had her students preparing and then lecturing the class instead of the faculty. Who thought of that?

Around the same time, I started an early morning session with my trainees in which they had to take a question pertaining to a patient that they had seen, research the topic, find evidentiary support, and then present their findings to the whole group, including faculty who specialized in that area. The process of questioning, researching, and presenting engaged my trainees in a way that no lecture ever could and the amount they were able to learn and apply was staggering.

This sparked my interest to learn more about learning from both a scientific perspective and from a pragmatic implementation standpoint. I soon had a chance to explore this further when I moved to Singapore and became Dean of the medical school.

In 2005, Duke and the government of Singapore entered into an agreement to create a new medical school there. This offered us an opportunity to develop a new way of learning based not on tradition but on what we know about the process. Professor Robert Kamei, who was training director of Paediatrics at University of California, San Francisco and Professor Sandy Cook imported the curriculum from Duke and shaped it into an innovative and effective delivery system called Team LEAD (LEAD =**Learn, Engage, Apply, Develop**).

The Art of Learning

This system required building goals for students, then giving them all the material that they needed to learn. Each class was devoted to assessing if they learnt the material, further discussion, and an exam. After a break, they had to use what they learnt to apply and solve problems based on case material from patients. You will soon see that this system uses many of the learning principles that you will encounter as you read this book.

As this was going on, I became more and more aware of how schools and universities seem stuck in a paradigm that does not work and seemed both unaware and unwilling to change.

So two years ago, I started to write short commentaries for a widely-circulated newspaper, *TODAY,* on learning and education. The commentaries were meant to raise awareness about learning, schooling, and educational systems. The response was tremendous and I was gratified by the level of interest and dialogue the series generated. [1]

Schoolteachers began to approach us about using the LEAD method to teach math and science classes. With a bit of adaptation a few of them have begun to use many of these principles, and now there has been an increasing level of interest in building and extending these learning principles to a whole range of educational settings, from schools to adult learning sites. Many of the teachers and faculty asked about where they can learn more and thus was born the conception of this book.

This book is my way of synthesizing what we know about learning from a scientific perspective to develop a set of learning principles to guide students and parents. Since we began using many of these principles early on at Duke and now in Singapore, we have become convinced of their universality and applicability to all learning.

---

[1]Published as a compilation: K. Ranga Rama Krishnan " How to Lead (Learn, Engage, Apply, Develop), Media Corp Press 2015 Singapore

These principles are derived from the science of learning. They are natural and seem to occur in many species not just amongst humans. They can be visualized for the most part as natural laws that are robust and established. They are enduring and permanent. The reality of many of these principles will become obvious as you move through the early chapters of the book. The laws or principles of learning are woven into the fabric of life and our learning, be it intentional or not, derives from this fact. There is not one principle in this book that is unique to any one age, gender, or subject. They are deeply fundamental and universally applicable. The more closely we comprehend and follow the learning principles, the better our knowledge and our ability to apply that understanding to learning.

How to Use this Book

My advice is to look at this book, not as something that you start from the beginning and finish at the end, but as a guide that you return to as you learn. You may choose to read through it completely the first time in order to get a picture of the whole, but you will get more value when you use it as you need it. One of the first principles that you will learn is that you will retain what you learn longer the more you use it and the more you connect that knowledge to what you already know. As you progress through these principles, many of them will appear natural and become second nature. Others, such as spacing and mixing up, will seem counter-intuitive at first but try the approach and you won't regret it.

These principles are not a set of discrete and unconnected formulas; they are part of a whole learning paradigm and the shift in how you learn. This new paradigm will feel strange at first, but when you apply it, you will see benefits that help promote and sustain the shift. The principles will bring long-term benefit to your learning and growth. The material is organized to be your learning companion as you move forward, grow, and learn. It is organized with specific ideas and guides that you can use to study and focus on whatever material that you need to become proficient in.

If you have friends or children that you want to guide, approach this material as a way to learn and teach. In fact the more you are able to digest, synthesize, and explain, the more you will learn. Read the material as if you have to explain it to your sceptical friend, spouse, or better yet another teacher. You will notice the difference in how you think about the material once you know you have to convince another individual.

Approach the material about each of the rules with an eye toward implementation. Then try it when it is fresh in your mind. And then try it again. The more you use what you learn here, the better you will retain it. As you progress, natural learning process will become even more natural and self-fulfilling.

Learning is Natural

The Learning Paradigm

"Tell me and I forget. Teach me and I remember.
Involve me and I learn."
— Benjamin Franklin

The Art of Learning

We constantly have thoughts, feelings, ideas, and sensations; some we are aware of, others we are not. Some of these ideas we can recall consciously and others require a trigger or an association. Other thoughts, ideas, and concepts come to mind spontaneously and involuntarily, often triggered by associations—some conscious and some not—that bring it to the fore.

Perception, memory, our internal thoughts, and individual learning are inextricably linked and difficult to dissemble. This living, constantly adapting connection leads to the accumulated experience of life that in turn leads to the interpretation and use of future knowledge.

Perception means becoming aware through our senses. Our ability to perceive sensory input is influenced by what we expect to see, hear, smell, or taste. Perceptions are swayed by prior knowledge of what the image, the sound, or the sensation is likely to be in its particular context. A wonderful book, *Why we see what we do: A Wholly Empirical Theory of Vision* by my colleague, Dale Purves, illustrates this with a world filled with illusions as our brain tries to predict and make sense of the environment that we live in.

Imagine an animal rushing toward you. From a distance it appears small, but it looms larger as it gets closer to you. Your brain is not fooled into thinking that the animal is growing as it approaches you because—thankfully—your perception is based on your existing knowledge.

Almost everything we "see" is not seen like a camera or a video recorder but is interpreted by the brain based upon prior knowledge; knowledge that is constantly modified by learning and storage in memory.

A number of acquired percepts (the mental result or impression or sensation of something perceived) illustrate this principle. For example, recognizing the notes in a musical piece, or the taste and smell of fine wine, or recognizing objects we have seen before.

An important feature in perception is constancy, the ability to identify the same object even with variable sensory inputs. We can distinguish individual people from different angles and views even though the projection of the image on the eye is very different. Although this does get difficult if the image is completely inverted. Try it yourself: turn the faces of people you know upside down and try to recognize them. You can do it but it requires more effort. Some of these percepts are easier to learn than others. As an example, we can distinguish better between individuals who are similar to us by race than those who are different from us. This makes sense given the critical nature of our ability to distinguish socially.

For perception to occur, attention is the essential ingredient. Not all stimuli in the perceptual field receive equal attention; only some stimuli are likely to reach the threshold of awareness, while others are ignored. If you were to walk into a room in search of a friend, your attention would be focused on your search rather than the objects in the room. It is unlikely you would notice whether the table had dust on it when you are looking for a person. Thus attention is the first step in perception. It functions like a "spotlight" that can illuminate only a restricted quantity of material, facilitating the perception of the stimuli of interest while sacrificing other details.

The sayings of Sherlock Holmes, the eponymous detective immortalized by Arthur Conan Doyle, is pertinent and timeless: "The world is full of obvious things which nobody by any chance ever observes." And "You see, but you do not observe. The distinction is clear." Our minds are designed to focus on points of interest and we do not "see" all things all the time[2].

---

[2]From the Adventures of Sherlock Holmes: A Scandal in Bohemia. This is a classic and telling quote.

The Art of Learning

We can only keep our focus on very few things at any given time. This focus is called *selective attention* and when we move our attention from one thing to the next, at least three steps have to take place:

1. Disengaging attention from one target;
2. Moving attention to the next target; and
3. Re-engaging attention on the new target.

Imagine walking into Wal-Mart looking for a particular brand microwave oven. First your attention will be focused on finding the kitchen electronics aisle, then you will move it to finding the microwave section; finally your attention will move to finding the particular brand you want. Each time you utilize the above three steps to find what you are looking for. One of the more lucid and vivid definitions of attention is by William James, who says attention "is the taking possession of the mind, in clear and vivid form, of one out of what may seem several simultaneously possible objects or trains of thoughts...It implies withdrawal from some things in order to deal effectively with others."

Attention

Learning

Perception

Memory

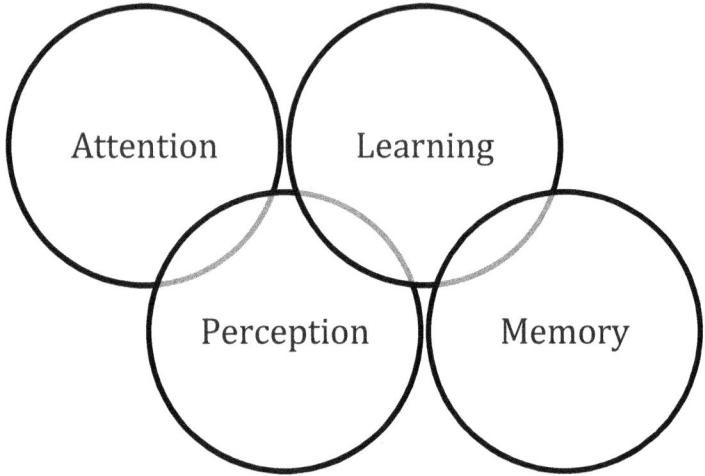

Our attention systems select vital or goal-relevant stimuli from the environment while ignoring or suppressing the processing of those stimuli—the distractors—that are not important.

Our brains are wired from the beginning for survival and these pertinent stimuli grab our attention immediately. The sudden instances of a ball flying toward you or the unexpected honk of a car are all stimuli that require immediate behavioural responses.

Biologically significant fear stimuli, such as snakes, spiders, and angry facial expressions draw our attention immediately. We find pictures of snakes and spiders more quickly in our visual field than flowers or trees. These attention-grabbing features are probably part of our evolutionary mechanism for survival, however most of our attention and thereby perception is influenced by learnt knowledge context and expectation.

How we feel and our interest conveys important information about our current priorities, and therefore attention and perception are tuned and oriented toward these priorities. We will

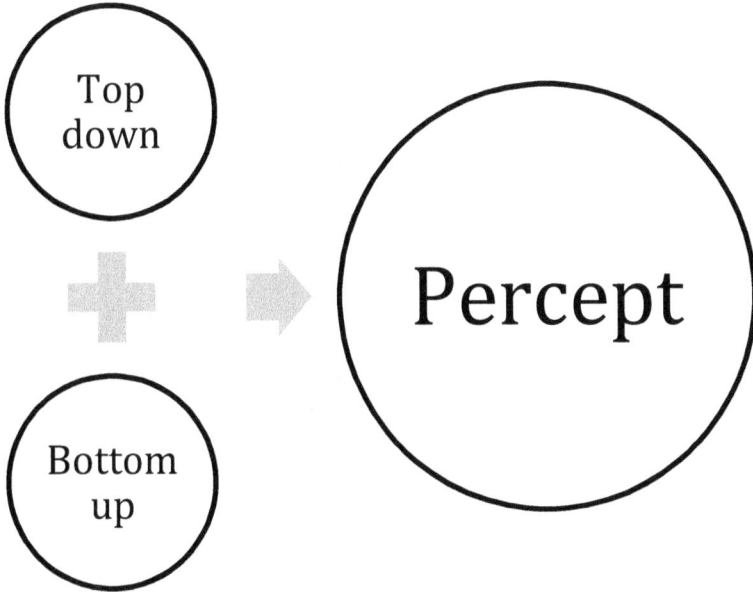

come back to this in following chapters. Without motivation and interest we will not direct attention to what we need to learn. Without attention we do not learn.

Imagine you are in a room and everyone is talking about shopping. If you hear the word "sail" you are likely to interpret it as "sale". Similarly, if we hear the word "male" while we are talking about delivery of books we are likely to interpret what we heard as "mail". Motivational and expectation bias can influence even concrete percepts. This influence from "above"—our knowledge and expectations—is called *top down processing*; when our brains evaluate information derived from our senses, it is referred to as *bottom up processing*. The convergence of these two types of processing leads to the percept.

The other element is Memory. Memories are the inner histories that we store and maintain. Since memory is contingent upon prior learning, the initial step occurs when our sensory systems send information to the brain. The first stage in memory is encoding. Think of it as putting things into a file cabinet. The second is storage and the third is retrieval, or extracting the stored information. It sounds very simple but it is not. Your brain is not like a video recorder. It does not store the information as is.

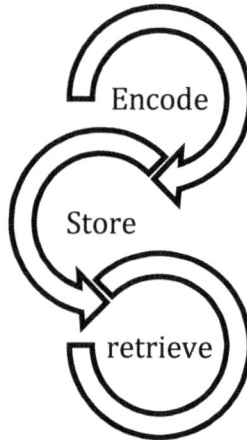

When we see or hear or taste something, our nervous system (the part that works with senses is called the sensory system) constructs a very transitory record of the stimuli. Sensory information that is stored is fleeting. Our sensory system can hold numerous items concurrently, but only transiently. Visual information is stored from about 0.1 to 0.3 seconds, while auditory information will be stored for about 1 to 4 seconds.

In the real world, we use all the sensory information to construct a perception of the event. The illusion of ventriloquism is based on the visual signalling of the sound. From our own individual experience we know that we are in a loud party where we cannot hear very well but seeing the person and their mouth and facial movements can enhance hearing by a significant amount.

Small experiments show the power of a sensory stimulation affecting another sense. When research volunteers were shown a single flash of light accompanied by two beeps they reported seeing two flashes. This is a sound induced flash illusion and seems to happen by changing perceptual sensitivity to light.

The Art of Learning

The next stage of the process is short-term memory. Let's say we are given a number to call in the next few minutes. That number can be held in our brain's short-term storage until we use it, and then unless we plan to reuse that number it is forgotten. Our brains provisionally hold the information. Short-term memory has limits, thus we cannot retain a large sequence of numbers. Phone numbers are manageable but a bank account number is much more difficult to remember.

The next step is to extract meaning from the percept by focusing on it long enough to consider transferring it into long-term memory. In this phase of memory establishment, the brain retains encoded data over long periods of time. This means it encodes the information in a stable way somewhere in the brain. Scientists have made progress in understanding long-term memory processes and how they work. Repeated stimuli with gaps between them lead to activating processes in key neurons. These lead to protein formation that strengthen connection between nerve cells and thus, it is believed, long-term storage of information. In an ingenious study, honeybees were monitored in order to contrast learning that happens all at once (cramming) and spaced learning shows the importance of having an interval between stimuli.[3]

What Can Honeybees Teach Us about Learning?

The honeybee is an interesting insect to choose to study learning and memory. Honeybees live in colonies and are social insects that need to return dependably to their colony for safety and shelter. The colonies can exist for very long times and need to continually evolve to cope with changing environmental conditions. Bees look for food (nectar) at many locations and they

---

[3]Menzel et al., 2001Menzel, R., Manz, G., Menzel, R., and Greggers, U. (2001). Massed and spaced learning in honeybees: the role of CS, US, the intertrial interval, and the test interval. Learn. Mem. 8, 198–208.

need to be able to learn spatial cues to help them return to their colony. Their brains are very small and it is indeed remarkable that they learn and engage and adapt to very diverse changing conditions with less than 1 million neurons.

An ingenious way to test their learning and memory is to study their response to sugar and nectar. When their taste buds are stimulated they extend their proboscis. This response is very reliable and easy to measure. We can test their learning by pairing with other stimuli both smell and vision. After multiple learning trials, memory gets consolidated and retained for several days. This long-term retention of memory is better with spacing.

Utilizing gaps between training stimuli of 30 seconds, 3 minutes, and 10 minutes, memory was then tested after 30 minutes, one day and three days. Honeybees trained with 30-second gaps showed the greatest learning around 30 minutes but this rapidly decreased, falling to 20% on the third day, an indication that only short-term memory had been produced. In contrast, honeybees trained with 10-minute gaps between learning trials showed less retention after 30 minutes but subsequently amalgamated and retained these memories, demonstrating long-term memories had been produced.

Spaced conditioning lead to more retention over a longer time than when conditioning happened at very short intervals. It is likely that you need time for consolidation of memory to occur and very short time intervals do not allow this to happen. From this work on honeybees and in other species including humans, many of the neurobiological principles that underlie learning, memory and the spacing effect is being teased out.

Long-Term Memory —Encoding, Storage, and Recall

A fascinating study of patients with severe epilepsy showed the formation of specific memory formation in single neurons, and was able to show facets of memory mechanisms in free recall.

Three periods of 16 five-seconds-long memorable video clips were presented to patients. Then, when the patient recalled the memory of the video, internally generated reactivation of single neurons involved in memory acquisition of a clip occurred during recall of that clip, signifying localization of some elements of memory in specific neurons.[4] A diverse range of images activated different groups of neurons that were encoding both abstract and basic properties of the images. This proposes memory processes that can encode in a way that structures complex information. The process has two stages: an early stage and then a later one that involves protein synthesis. This later stage process is how memory is retained longer.

Memory storage for the long term involves not just one neuron or one set of neurons but more often a distributed network. Memory consolidation describes the formation of long-term memory that is spread across many regions of the brain.It is thought to involve reorganization over time of the brain systems that encode the memory, and in the course of this the storage of memory may spread to new places in the brain while at the same time abandoning its need on the parts of the circuits that have served its acquisition.

Besides spacing there has been growing evidence that learning by interposing different tasks helps with longer-term retention. In real life we are unlikely to be engaged in just one activity at a time. We are more than likely to be switching between different tasks even in what appears to be routine day-to-day life, such as shopping. Tasks have to be interrupted, switched around, stopped, and restarted. It appears that when tasks are learnt via interposing tasks it takes a longer time to learn but retention is longer.

---

[4](Gelbard-Sagiv et al., 2008Gelbard-Sagiv, H., Mukamel, R., Harel, M., Malach, R., and Fried, I. (2008). Internally generated reactivation of single neurons in human hippocampus during free recall. Science 322, 96–101. doi: 10.1126/science.1164685).

This may be because it promotes greater integration of task memories and system consolidation of memories. Imaging studies of the brain have shown that interweaving tasks show changes in the brain consistent with taking a longer time to learn and a better retention of memories. In other words, we learn by mixing it up.[5]More parts of the brain are engaged, indicating greater use of the brain system.

When this learning is linked to what we already know, it is stored longer. Psychologists call this connection to pre-existing knowledge *the principle of elaboration*. In fact, we do this all the time. We may have a hard time recollecting isolated facts, but if the facts are linked to what we already know we are far more likely to remember them.

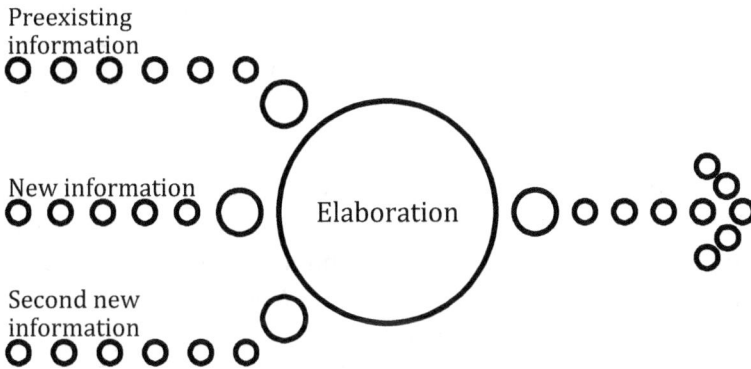

[5]Lin, C.H., Knowlton, B.J., Chiang, M.C., Iacoboni, M., Udompholkul, P., & Wu, A.D. (2011). Brain–behavior correlates of optimizing learning through interleaved practice. *Neuro Image, 56*(3), 1758–1772.

We remember even better when we relate what we learn to each other, a feat that requires us to organize the material (organization principle) in our own minds. We have a vast capacity for storing memory. Indeed we can store an entire lifetime of memories. Information is broken into elements and pieces of our experiences and is retained in a manner to allow us to recreate experiences and events when needed. Keep in mind that these recreations are not exact. We can mix things up or perceive it differently depending on merely the time and situation we find ourselves in.

Even though we are constantly bombarded with information, only a very limited amount is committed to long-term storage. It is particularly important to note that we cannot remember information that we failed to perceive and then encode for memory storage in the first place. Once the essentials of an event or an experience are classified, each part is shunted to a different brain region for a comparison and evaluation for perceptible similarities to previously stored knowledge or information begins.

The various pieces of new information get stored by modifying existing knowledge in neural circuits distributed throughout the cerebral cortex. Our brains consolidate material into networks based on conceptual classes. My memory of how to use an ophthalmoscope is perhaps linked to my knowledge of the eye, memories of particular eye disease, etc. We do not know all the different categories but because of studies in humans who have had brain damage we can infer regions of the brain that specialize in using tools and recognizing faces.

This style of organization explains why people who suffer injuries to small parts of the brain can lose very specific knowledge. One may lose memories of animals, which are often learned by their appearance, but not of tools, which are often learned by how they are used.

The Art of Learning

Once the material is stored we need to be able to access and retrieve it in order to use it. Cues help pull knowledge from our memory banks. That is why multiple-choice tests are easier than tests that are based on free recall. Tests of recall are indeed better learning tools but they are harder to build and administer if they have to be given to large numbers of participants.

Prompts or cues work best when they are linked to the context in which the material was learnt, that is either by subject matter or by location. If the material that is being encoded is linked to as many contexts as possible then many different cues can help retrieve the material.

An interesting observation is that retrieval is aided by anticipation so if students were expecting a multiple choice test and are instead asked free response questions, they will not do as well. The opposite is also true.

Retrieval and encoding reinforce each other and constitute a positive feedback loop.

Every time you recall effectively you are re-encoding. The more you test, especially by free recall, the better the long-term storage and better the subsequent ease of recall. Testing is a powerful mode of learning.

In fact, testing before someone learns the material will enhance memory for that material. This is called *the testing effect.* Even just trying to recall what we already know—even if we do not know the answer—helps retain the material when we actually learn it.

To quote Sherlock Holmes:

"I consider that a man's brain originally is like a little empty attic, and you have to stock it with such furniture as you choose. A fool takes in all the lumber of every sort that he comes across, so that the knowledge which might be useful to him gets crowded out, or at best is jumbled up with a lot of other things, so that he has a difficulty in laying his hands on it. Now the skilful workman is very careful indeed as to what he takes into his brain-attic. He will have nothing but the tools which may help him in doing his work, but of these he has a large assortment, and all in the most perfect order. It is a mistake to think that little room has elastic walls and can distend to any extent. Depend upon it - there comes a time when for every addition of knowledge you forget something that you knew before. It is of the highest importance, therefore, not to have useless facts elbowing out the useful ones[6]."

It is indeed a very valuable perspective. What we read, watch, and believe influences what else we decide to read, watch, and believe in. If we allow our mind to be closed we will end up reinforcing beliefs and lose our ability to see what does not fit. In essence, we will lose our ability to learn, store, and recall new information in both the short- and long-term.

In addition to short- and long-term memory storage, our memory is also defined by what we are tasked with remembering. Psychologists commonly categorize memory into that which we can recall consciously, namely facts, figures, people, information, and events (also called *declarative memory*). That which we cannot consciously recall or be aware of, such as sports, procedural skills, habits, and reactions, we remember without conscious effort (*non-declarative memory*).

Types of Memory

Declarative memory could be memory for facts or memory for events and experiences. The word "semantic" is used to

---

[6]Available as: *A Study in Scarlet* at Project Gutenberg.

describe memory for facts (e.g. names of elements, names of cities) and "episodic" for events and experiences (e.g. autobiographical information, people, such as whom my teacher was in first grade). Episodic memory has information that includes a time, location, and nature of the event.

Declarative memory is also called *conscious memory*. It is what we talk about when we describe learning at school in terms of subjects such as math, science etc. This memory is used to build a conscious model of the world and concepts that help us make sense of the world. It is conscious memory that is so detrimentally impacted by amnesia. Amnesia affects the ability to retrieve past memories (also called retrograde amnesia), or the ability to form new memories (anterograde amnesia), or both.

Non-declarative memory does not enter our consciousness at all. It consists of habits and skills such as riding a bike, driving a car, or learning to stitch. This type of memory for skills is often called *procedural memory*. The biology underlying procedural memory is distinct from memory that is conscious, and therefore people can develop amnesia but be perfectly fine with skills that they learnt or vice versa. Procedural memory can be motor skills, (mental) knowledge of rules and procedure, or a combination of the two. Most of what we do like driving to work involves a combination of both procedural memory—the driving skill—and declarative memory—where we are going and the rules of the road.

Amnesic patients can also usually learn new skills. Those facts demonstrate that declarative and procedural memories use different systems within the brain.

There are two additional phenomena related to memory that is not overtly conscious. One is *conditioning*, which is the process of procuring the kind of information that leads to an automatic response. Ivan Pavlov's classic experiments are a perfect example. Pavlov taught dogs to associate the ringing of a bell with a food.

Eventually the dogs would salivate at the sound of a bell, even when the food is not presented. The second is *priming*. Priming refers to an event or experience helping recall of another event. An example of priming is if one reads a list of words including the word *"neutral"* and is later requested to complete a word starting with *"neu"* the likelihood that they will answer *"neutral"* is more than if they were not primed. Amnesic patients can retain the capacity to demonstrate a priming effect.

Emotions modulate memories and we remember negative and arousing events better than boring ones. Emotional memories and their attendant features have been best studied in the context of development of fears and in human's phobia. They involve regions of the brain that are quite distinct from those involved with learning skills or events. Emotional memory can be conscious or could be sub- or unconscious.

In real life, we use all these memory systems at the same time, in parallel and usually integrated. A soloist preparing for a performance mentally replays the melody (conscious or declarative memory), then reviews details about the forthcoming event and practices the song with other members of the band (procedural memory). A football player remembers the plays and knows when a particular play is called (declarative memory) and then executes the play based on the skills that he has learnt in practice (procedural memory).

After the memory is consolidated, new data can cause a memory to change, strengthen, or weaken. The memory may not be completely accurate. Just like with perception, our minds in trying to make sense will fill in or alter details. Retrieval is when we fetch enduring information out of memory back for usage. Thus, retrieving a memory is rarely exact.

From this perspective, learning is a matter of modifying information in memory using new knowledge input or experiences.

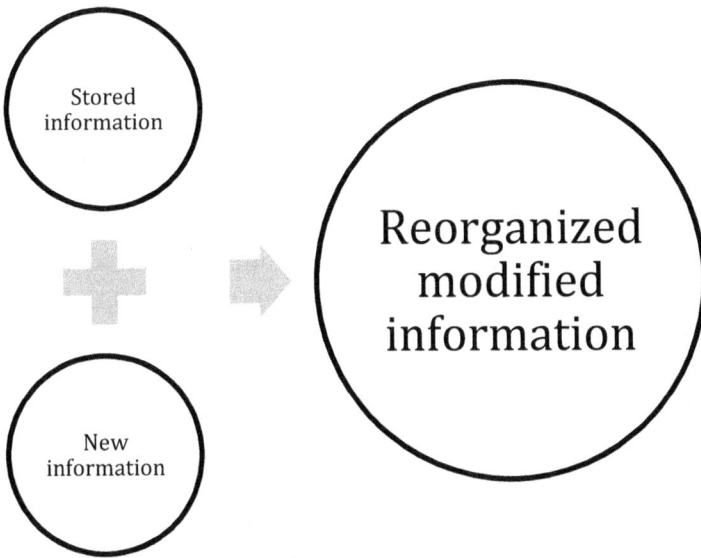

How and Why Memory Strength Varies

Memory is fluid and the brain revisits and reorganizes stored data through a repetitive updating procedure. Prior understanding is revised based on new information and sometimes changed beyond recognition. This process results from the frequent conscious and subconscious occurrence of memories, thoughts, and ideas that facilitate the interpretation and understanding of new experiences. This is not fettered by the fact that the factors constituting the prior experience are not necessarily in consciousness.

Thus, memory is an ever-adapting representation and malleable guide to the environment. Memory does not have to be conscious or explicit. Most of what we learn at school is explicit, but much of what we learn in our day-to-day life is implicit. Often, we are not even aware of what we learnt. In fact many habits, such as drinking coffee with a certain cup at a certain time, or even many biases such as how we like or dislike someone can develop without our awareness. This implicit memory is not a focus of this book but indeed is a topic of great interest on its own merit.

There is extraordinary diversity in how individuals learn in this respect! One person may remember well, while another has a poor ability for recollection. This is true not only when comparing across individuals but also for the same individual in different phases of time (morning and evening) and age (young versus old). Memory also varies by content; some can remember music and songs easily but are remarkably forgetful for other things. All of this varies greatly by the individual. Finally, the intensity of the attention and interest attached to the content can determine how well it is remembered too. The pain of touching a hot stove or the fire is a one-shot experience seared into memory.

When first exposed to any new material or knowledge, we establish new neural networks—of the words, images, sounds, etc.—to represent this novel experience. However, upon being exposed to the same material even in a different format or location or by another person on a second occasion, it reactivates established connections with recognition.

Memory is like taking a picture or recording a sound and ripping it up into tiny pieces and putting the pieces in different cubbyholes. The memory is then rebuilt from the individual fragments of the memory.

Memory Triggers, Chains, and the Learning Curve

We continually take in and store new information, by updating, retrieving, using, and restoring existing memory information.

The Art of Learning

Let's say you are giving a talk at a conference and you hear a gentleman speak in an earlier panel. You recognize his voice, and then you recognize his face, recalling that you grew up with him as a child. Then you remember your stories from that time. This is a typical chain of events recalled after a trigger. This chain uses many pieces of memory, pulling from both types. The mechanism involves modifications of brain physiology and even structure by experience.

Now you can see how habits are formed. Reinforcing learning—by repetition and, in many cases, by reward—forms habits. Habit development is the route by which new behaviours become programmed. If you instinctively reach for a smoke the instant you wake up in the morning, you have a habit (albeit an unhealthy one). By the same principle, if you feel inclined to get up, stretch and exercise, you've acquired a healthy habit. The habit pathways are reinforced and etched into our brain. Our habits are often formed by positive reinforcement; much addictive behaviour starts with a bit of reward. Habits require less energy from your brain by making the response routine. For both animals and humans the design for simplicity in response is through the development of habits. When we start to learn a new behaviour the process involves effort and training, but at a point it becomes unconscious and programmed. This new behaviour is then reinforced by rewards and diminished by punishment. Habits and patterned ways of behaviour imbue our personality.

The Learning Curve

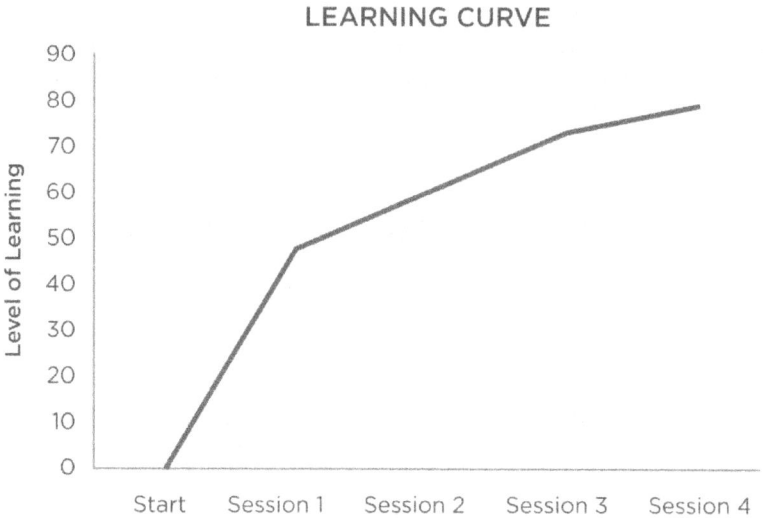

LEARNING CURVE

The Learning curve is just a plot of learning a task or skill against time.

If you plot the time it takes to learn a game, you will likely see that the initial phase of learning is steep. Then, over subsequent periods, the rate of learning slows. This pattern is seen for almost all forms of learning, from playing a sport or a piece of music to learning science or math. The rate or slope of the learning may vary both by individual ability and the type of skill that is being learnt.

The Art of Learning

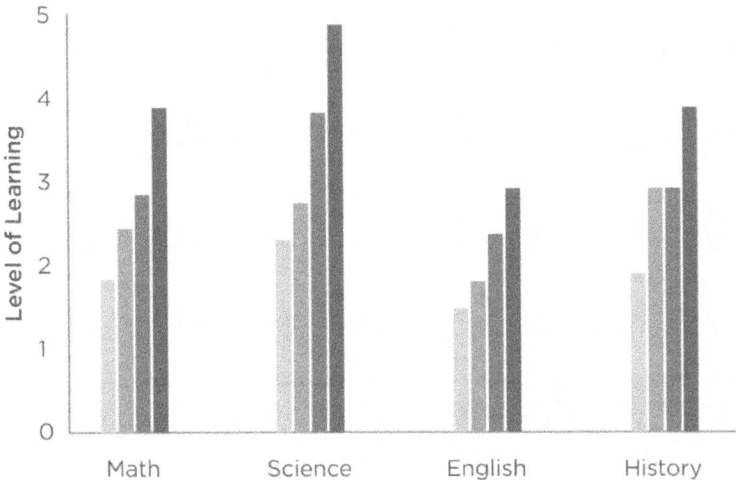

The learning curve for each subject could have a different shape based on ability, interest, motivation etc.

If the task is difficult the rate of change will follow a similar pattern but the slope may be shallower.

The main reason for building learning curves is to see if particular methods of learning change the slope of learning. The curves look smooth when plotted for a group of individuals but can look erratic when it is plotted for just one person.

The learning principle is simple: Repetition of the same action or material makes us remember the action better with less time or effort expended on that process. It becomes more automatic and less conscious.

The pattern of learning can vary from individual to individual on a given task even if the trajectory pattern is similar. It can also vary for the same individual across different tasks. We know this from our own experience in learning. Some tasks simply seem easier than others.

LEARNING CURVE FOR DIFFERENT INDIVIDUALS

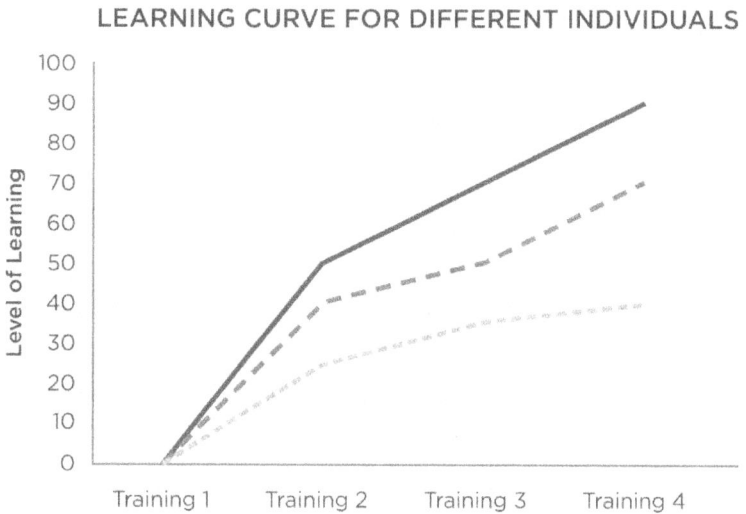

What may seem counterintuitive is that the more difficult the learning task is, the longer the memory for the material will remain.

A Princeton study presented learning material in two formats, one was an easy to read format that was familiar ("Arial") and the other was in an uncommon font ("Comic Sans").Students who read the text in the more difficult format remembered better than those who read in the easy format. It is possible that the increased difficulty in reading led to more attention, and therefore better retention of the material.[7]

Learning and Forgetting

---

[7](Diemand-Yauman, C., et al. Fortune favors the ( ): Effects of disfluency on educational outcomes. Cognition (2010),)
http://web.princeton.edu/sites/opplab/papers/Diemand-Yauman_Oppenheimer_2010.pdf

The Art of Learning

This brings up a key obstacle to learning: Forgetting. What do we know about forgetting? The classic example is the self-study by Ebbinghaus, which set the stage for memory research. He wanted to study how long it takes one to forget something he previously learned. What is the relationship between the amount of time you study and the length of time that you can remember what you learnt?

Ebbinghaus carried out an extensive almost obsessive set of studies to answer his questions. First he created a list of 2000-plus nonsense words, each consisting of one vowel and several consonants. He then carried out a series of experiments on himself in which he memorized 8 lists of 13 words and then waited for some time before testing his recollection and studying them again. He tested his recollection over a variety of time intervals—20 minutes, 1hour, 9 hours,1 day, 2 days, 6 days and 31 days.

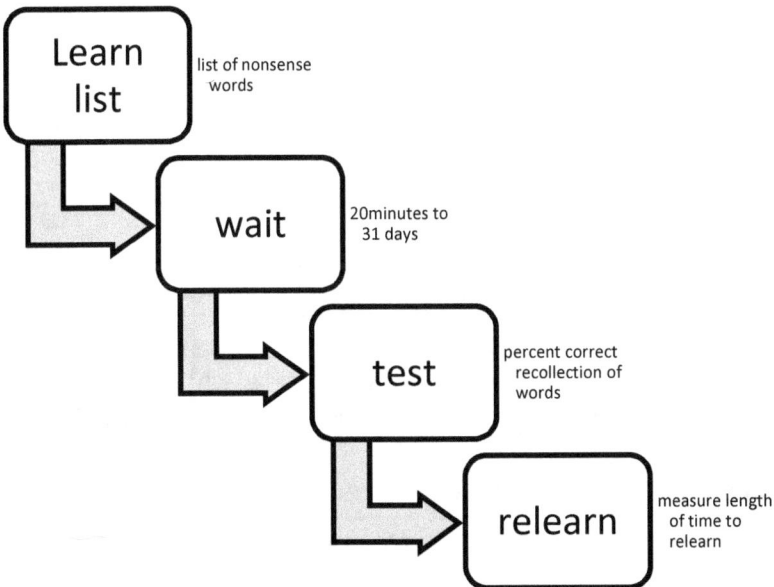

Learn list — list of nonsense words

wait — 20minutes to 31 days

test — percent correct recollection of words

relearn — measure length of time to relearn

He calculated the time it took him to relearn the list each time and then recorded it as a percentage of the original time that it took him to learn the list. He found that the rate of forgetting was steep. In 20 minutes only 58% of the original learning was saved; in 1week only 25% was saved.

The forgetting curve

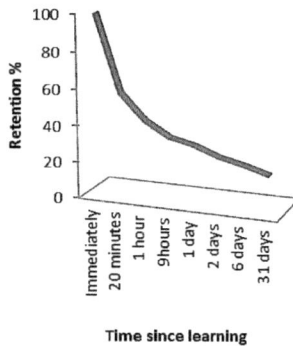

Ebbinghaus' study shows that memory for non-contextualized information is very short and can drop off dramatically over a relatively short period of time.

The second important insight was that repetition improved retention. To quote Ebbinghaus: "The effect of the repetitions is at first approximately constant, the saving in work which results from these repetitions increases accordingly for a while proportional to their number. Gradually the effect becomes less; and finally, when the series has become so firmly fixed that it can be repeated almost spontaneously after 24 hours, the effect is shown to be decidedly less."

This is the classic description of the learning curve.

In addition, repetitions that were spread over greater time intervals worked better than if the repetitions were all done at the same time. This is called *spaced learning* and has been used in various programs to improve vocabulary, such as the Pimsleur method. For many experiences, frequent repetition is what makes it possible to remember large blocks of information. Reading once does not learn vocabularies, multiplication tables, rhymes and poems generally. Their mastery is ensured only by multiple repetitions.

But the phrase, "Use it or lose it," certainly applies.

When learned material is not tapped and used, the ability to recall content is lost under the influence of time. The most common way in which students learn is geared towards taking and passing examinations. Students pull all-nighters and cram facts right up until the final moments before examination time. This type of content vanishes fast because it is not grounded by conceptual understanding and later subjected to review. In other words, *He who crams fast forgets fast*. The amount of knowledge that is understood conceptually leads to the ability to use, analyse, synthesize, and build. The more the knowledge is used, the more it is retained and helps to grow other knowledge.

Memory and retention is a key ingredient in learning. But even deeply ingrained content like one's mother tongue is impaired if not used for an extended time. I can attest to that from my own personal experiences.

This short-lived nature of memory clearly points the need for educational methods to keep this fact in mind to promote retention of material. Although memory remains an important component of learning we will discuss why understanding concepts and using them promotes more effective learning in the pages to come. The important thing to remember is that if you want to actually learn do not try to do it all at once.

The Art of Learning

Learning causes significant, enduring changes in the brain, in areas once believed to be immutable. Learning is an actual physical process in which new information forms new connections and strengthens existing connections when relearning happens. The connections formed in the brain are both functional and overtime structural in nature. The interested reader can delve into this fascinating theme by exploring some of the suggested reading.

Learning is a combination of integrated and seamless elements—from attention to perception to memory and retention—that makes us who we are and how we view the world and ourselves.

The Art of Learning

What does this mean for us as a student? How can we use what we know about the science of learning to help us learn?

The rapid progress of scientific understanding in this area tells us how memory learning and even habits are formed and how learning processes shapes our personality. But what we are interested in is how to use what we know to increase our ability to learn.

The key principles we can derive from the science of learning are:

1. First, we learn by paying attention. Therefore, motivation and interest become key drivers in directing our mind's focus to what we want and need to learn.

2. Second, repeated practice is an essential element for long-term storage. In order for memory to be retained for long spans of time, the information or skill requires repeated practice.

3. Learning is faster when we learn all at once (*massed learning*) than when we learn with sessions paced over time. But memory is better stored when the learning happens in multiple sessions, spaced over time, rather than all at once. So if you need to study for a test that is tomorrow, cramming is okay provided that you will not need to remember the material three weeks later. If you need to store that information for the long term, greater spacing is needed.

4. Learning is faster when we learn one skill at a time, but we remember better and for a longer time if we learn skills interspersed with one another rather than sequentially. We also learn when to use which skill for what situation. This seems cumbersome but you will see practical ways to do so. So if you have to study math, intermixing solved problems with problems to solve can make it easier to learn. Interspersing topics is another great way to consolidate memory: study a bit of science, then history and math rather than one topic every day.

5. Learning is better reinforced when it is connected to what we already know. Thus establishing connections by elaborating, organizing information, and summarizing can improve retention and better application of what we learn. How do we do it? Right after you learn a topic, reflect and see how you can connect it to what you already know.

6. Habits, both good and bad, can form over time; reinforcement makes habit formation faster.

7. Finally, we are built to learn. We learn all the time. If we allow our curiosity to drive learning by discovery we will be the better for it.

Learning Language

A specific example of learning: How do we learn languages?

Learning a language is no simple feat. It is something that can all too often take years of intensive study. So how do we learn language and what can happen when something in the process goes wrong?

Human language is made up of two sounds—consonants and vowels. A consonant is a sound that we produce by partially closing one part of our vocal apparatus (the lips or the tongue, palate etc.) Vowels are the sounds that are produced by a comparatively open vocal tract. More than 600 consonants and 200 vowels have been identified as being used in human languages. These consonants and vowels vary according to language, region, or even dialect.

Most languages have about forty sounds called phonemes. These are non-identical units of sound that are used in language. When a baby is born, it can hear and discriminate these various phonemes as long as its hearing apparatus is intact and functional. But what the baby hears will become a learned pattern that is shaped by the language of the household. For example, the baby will hear more Tamil in a Tamil household or English in an English-speaking house. The more it hears a particular set of phonemes, it learns to focus and discriminate between those it commonly hears and others. The baby figures out the set of phonemes that it has to learn.

This narrowing of focus happens within the first year of life amongst most infants. Thus in an English-speaking household the baby will show greater identification and differentiation of English phonemes than would a baby in a Mandarin speaking home.

These auditory experiences become stored in memory and are the foundation of language development as the baby begins to relate the pattern of phonemes to objects and, over time, to tasks. When the baby slowly attempts to talk and mimic the sounds that it hears, it uses these memories to drive the vocal apparatus until it is able to match the sound. Interestingly, even a baby's babble corresponds to the common phonemes (and thus the language) of the household.

What about Reading?

When I am reading an article, I typically only see just a few words at a time, often no more than two or three. How does our brain process these words and make sense of what the words mean? The part of the brain that extracts information from the image is able to identify shapes. It is these shape recognition systems that are present in animals and humans that we use for recognizing the visual identification of words and symbols.

Whenever we read and in whatever language, whether it is Hindi or Mandarin or English, the same brain networks are activated. Imaging studies have shown a region in the base of the back of the left side of the brain is the location where word recognition happens. In fact we have known for a hundred years that this special part of the brain is key for recognizing symbols and words. When that area is damaged by illness or injury the person cannot read words. (Alexia = cannot read words) Children who are poor readers do not activate this region of the brain to the same extent as good readers.

In an interesting study of this region of the brain amongst illiterates, it was found that this region activated with objects and faces unlike literates where the activation was more with words. In other words the reading took over a brain function that was previously related to facial recognition.

The Art of Learning

When we are born, our brain does not discriminate between left and right mirror images there is no need to visualize objects in the real world but for reading we have to discriminate between letters like b and d or between p and q. Illiterate individuals cannot discriminate and cannot tell the letters. We know this phenomenon in the primate world where we can show that the brain signal elicited by a shape is also elicited by its mirror image. In literate humans when a word and its mirror word are shown they are seen as separate and the brain signals are also different.

So in acquiring literacy, we acquire the ability to discriminate mirror images of letters and words. This again involves the same region of the brain. Acquiring the ability to read is accompanied by changes to the brain functions in this region.

We know that the image is recognized instantaneously as a sound and also for what it means. The brain circuits that are involved include the circuits that are those that process sounds and for recognizing spoken language and ascribing meaning to the words. In other words the image now has a sound and a meaning representation. The circuits that recognize the sound are different from that which recognizes meaning. Reading activates the same language circuits that spoken language does and now vision by reading gives access to a whole new world of information. It makes those circuits more sensitive to learning. Thus reading and learning a language are intimately related.

So given the complex process, it is no surprise that some children have difficulty reading. In a language like English the written representation and the phoneme can vary and just recognizing the phoneme may not be enough. We can tell from the difficulty that voice recognition programs have with 100% conversion of speech to text. Thus for many languages the problem can be poor learning of their phoneme and this could reflect that the culling of their ability to recognize the entire phonemes, to that which is relevant for the language could be a problem. It could also be difficulty with building the written script and linking it to the phoneme. In English some of this difficulty could relate to persistence of the mirror invariance. Today imaging studies and careful assessment can be used to understand the different problems underlying dyslexia. The data with dyslexia in Mandarin is more complicated. In Mandarin the individual characters are linked directly to the word or syllable and not to the phoneme. Thus suggestion that dyslexia in

Mandarin could be not just due to phonological problems but also minor visual deficits. Unfortunately studies in languages other than English are very limited.

What does this mean for helping students learn languages?

Learning a language requires intact hearing and phoneme identification. This starts in childhood and is natural.

1. It is good to speak with babies and speak around them. This fosters development of phoneme recognition.
2. If the child hears more than one language at a time, the child has to recognize more phonemes and it may take a bit longer to pick up the language. No need to get worried.
3. Reading and learning languages are intimately related. So phonics programs can be useful if children have trouble learning English.
4. For Mandarin and related languages in which the word is directly related to the character, reading difficulty could stem from more reasons than simply phonic recognition.
5. Language forms the basis for all other forms of learning. Therefore, if there is marked impairment in learning languages and reading it is worthwhile to have the child examined by specialists.

The Art of Learning

Learning numbers: Another special case of learning. How do we learn to count and calculate?

Building Number Sense

Let's say we are walking down a street and we see a shop selling t-shirts. If we choose to, we can determine at a glance how many shirts are being sold—one, two, three, or four. As the numbers get larger, say 11 or 12, it becomes difficult to say precisely how many shirts are being sold with just a glance. Instead, we have to count them.

This intuitive ability to judge quantities is called *number sense*. It is a useful and necessary tool for knowing how many objects are in our visual space, a skill shared by both humans and animals. A simple experiment that illustrates this is to ask, "Which number is bigger?" Then measure the time it takes to answer. When the difference between the two numbers is sizeable (i.e. 2 and 9), the lag time is much shorter than it is when the value of each number is similar (i.e. 8 and 9). The bigger the numbers are, the more time it takes to determine the difference (i.e. 1,748 and 1,784). This difficulty suggests that our brains have two mechanisms: one for precisely judging small numbers and the other for approximating magnitude when the numbers are large. We are all born with a number sense and this ability is present even in babies.

When babies are shown a continuous flow of images with each showing four objects arranged differently from one image to another, the baby gets bored and distracted. When a new image containing either a smaller or larger number of objects is shown then the baby perks up and is attentive again. This is very suggestive of a number sense and also a sensitivity to change in number. Babies have limits as to what they can distinguish and this is related to their age. Six-month-old babies can differentiate 8 versus 16 but not smaller differences; when they are 9 months old they can distinguish smaller differences; and when they are a year old, they will have a sense of decreasing and increasing counts.

In today's world, Arabic numerals are the most common way to represent numbers. The system has a base of 10, corresponding to the number of fingers in our two hands; fingers that we can use to count numbers. The way we count verbally is based on language; English uses more words to represent numbers up to twenty than Mandarin, whose words follow the same syntax as Arabic numeral representations. Interestingly that connects to younger Chinese speaking children counting to 40 by age 4 versus a much smaller number for English speaking children; and Cantonese speakers can hold up to 10 numbers in working memory compared to 7 for English language speakers.

As children develop verbal skills, they translate the counting "number sense" to words and symbols and gradually learn to manipulate them. But about 6% of children have trouble with math and difficulty applying mathematical concepts. This difficulty is labelled dyscalculia (trouble with calculation). In many such instances this appears to be failure in development or incomplete development of the number sense.

Poor number sense at a young age is a predictor of difficulty with math later on. Children who have trouble distinguishing between quantities do badly in arithmetic and continue to have difficulty with math as they grow up. Thus programs have been devised to improve number sense.

Recently, Number Sense games have been introduced to see if they can improve counting skills in young children who have difficulty with math. One of these is a game called Dots to Track. The game teaches children to connect the number of dots to the right Arabic numeral. When the children enter the wrong value the game prompts the children to add if the number is lower or remove dots if their number is higher to achieve the correct answer. The repeated practice with the game is designed to improve number sense.

Another **game** called Number Racer and Number Catcher also try to improve counting and increase connectivity with other elements of learning to foster the fundamental number sense.

This research into how we learn to count has had a remarkable bearing on our understanding math learning and offers guidance in helping children with math difficulty. The most important lesson is that learning math needs number sense and the earlier problems with number sense are identified, there maybe training options to improve math skills - skills that are essential in this world. A fascinating book by Stanislas Dehaene called *Number Sense* is a wonderful read on this subject.

What does this mean for students to learn math?

1. Learning math is an ability that requires the innate ability to count, known as number sense.
2. If the child demonstrates difficulty with number sense and math, it is worth evaluating early on.
3. If the problem is identified early, simple programmes and games like Number Racer can help.

Motivation- The Foundation of Learning

"Twenty years from now you will be more disappointed by the things that you didn't do than by the ones you did do, so throw off the bowlines, sail away from safe harbour, and catch the trade winds in your sails. Explore, Dream, Discover. "
–Mark Twain

Motivate

The word "motivate" means to be moved to an action. In learning as in most things in life, motivation is the prime key to success. Learners who have no motivation to learn a particular topic generally do not fare well. Those with a strong sense of motivation are far more likely to succeed.

Let's explore what motivation is and how to drive and sustain it.

Motivation is a multimodal phenomenon consisting of three key features: the **intensity** or strength of the motivating force; the **subject** of your motivation; and the **orientation**, or the "why" of it.

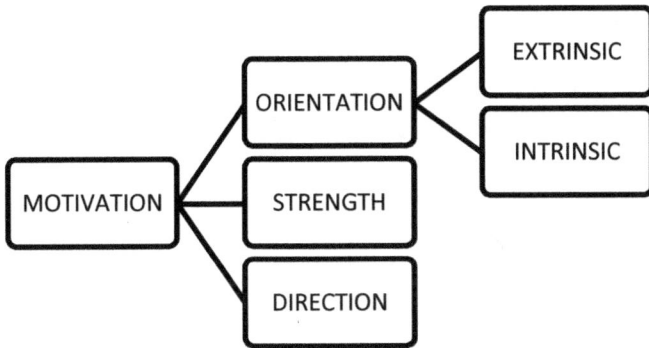

Motivation can vary; it can be transient or sustained and can change in intensity and strength.

We see it all the time when we raise children, when they show an inkling of an interest and maybe even when they have none, we send them for piano lessons, maybe a bit of violin, what about tennis, or Kumon for math. Soon we see the child lose interest, motivation and fusses when it comes time to go, but now they want to try soccer, guitar and so on and so forth. Attention and motivation can be very transient till something hooks the person to stick with their interest.

Why the direction of interest? Orientation of motivation looks at the why of action. It is founded on the primary attitudes and aims that give rise to interest and engagement. A learner can be motivated by inquisitiveness and curiosity or, because he or she wants approval or support or because of fear of punishment or losing face.

Intrinsic and extrinsic

Motivation that is driven by the student's interest is very different from when motivation is due to external reasons like a parent's approval. The motivation that is driven by innate desire and or interest is called intrinsic motivation. Intrinsic self-driven motivation is performance of an action for its inherent gratification rather than for an outside consequence. A self-motivated person acts for the joy or challenge required rather than because of losses or rewards due to outside factors.

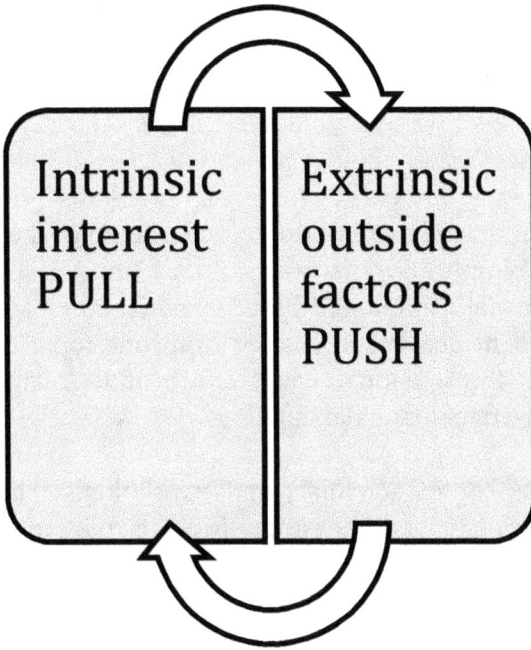

| Intrinsic interest PULL | Extrinsic outside factors PUSH |

This intrinsic or self-directed motivation is not just a human phenomenon but one that is seen in the animal realm in the form of lively and inquisitive behaviours and play without any expectation of reward.

Traditional theories of learning posited two laws. The first is the law of readiness, that is learning is invigorated by a motivational state such as hunger or thirst or desire for rewards, money, or recognition (all external factors); and the second Law is the law of effect, where learning was reinforced by rewards that satisfied the original motive. Intrinsic reasons were not believed to be important. But this view has changed. The inner pull of intrinsic motivation is very strong.

The Art of Learning

Daniel Berlyne, an American psychologist known for his work in exploratory behaviour, highlighted epistemic curiosity as a key facet of intrinsic motivation. Epistemic (from the Greek "episteme" for knowledge) curiosity is the "desire for knowledge that motivates individuals to learn new ideas, eliminate information-gaps, and solve intellectual problems". In other words, we are driven by an innate desire to make sense of the world we are born into. Simply *not knowing* drives this desire. Epistemic curiosity is usually provoked by an experience of ambiguity, it is usually transient and it can change from one topic to another but when it stirs the passion it takes a life of its own and leads to greater knowledge and understanding.

A number of scientists and psychologists have observed epistemic curiosity and the strength of its motivational force in creatures great and small:

Rats that cross electrical grids

The incredible amount of activity spent by rats in "exploring" a fresh situation can hardly escape the notice of anybody working with rats in the laboratory. When one of these animals is moved to another cage or when it moved back to its old cage the rat occupies a substantial length of time in a rushed but thorough survey of his surroundings. Even a hungry rat will forego food until it explores a new environment.

In a series of classical experiments conducted in the 1930's Henry W. Nissen, an experimental scientist known for his careful and thorough observation studies, showed that rodents would cross an electrified grid just to get a chance to explore a maze. Nissen tested and observed what would later be known as the Obstruction Method: A cluster of rats was given the chance to cross an electrified grid in order to explore a new maze or environment. He then compared his observations with another group of rats, who were very familiar with the environment on the other side of the grid and for whom the novelty factor was relatively immaterial. When they had a chance to explore a novel maze the animals crossed the electrified grid more than when they were familiar with what was on the other side. These studies showed that novelty and new environments serve as powerful incentives to promote behaviour. The rats were motivated by an inner pull—the desire to explore rather than a primary drive like hunger. Nissen found that even a well fed animal still wanted to explore. Rats would learn to press a lever just to get a chance to explore new surroundings. In these instances, the animals' motivation was purely intrinsic.

Monkeys with a monkey wrench

The primate psychologist Harry Harlow established a primate colony at University of Wisconsin-Madison. Known for his work studying dependency needs and social isolation in rhesus monkeys, Harlow also studied a number of primate behaviours and was surprised to see that primates would solve mechanical puzzles for no reward at all just for the heck of it. Monkeys would learn tasks just for the reward of looking at moving toys or even to just look at the experimental room from the outside. Novelty and the chance to explore were powerful stimuli for learning and were rewards that were intrinsic by themselves.

This same novelty and curiosity is an innate characteristic of humans. At birth human babies are active, curious, ready to learn and discover. The whole world is new to them and the need to explore and learn is not only a part of their nature, but a necessary element for survival. This attention to novelty—discovery learning—is the vital factor to the braingrowth and cognitive development that will shape the child's ability to live. As we get older this discovery learning fades for many individuals and the motivation that is driven by discovery and curiosity diminishes if we let it. Losing this motivation can quickly and detrimentally impact our overall health.

There is a very classic and telling experiment by Bexton, Heron, and Scott, in which participants were paid generously to do absolutely nothing, see nothing, hear very little, for 24 hours a day. They were almost entirely isolated[i] but well fed and well paid, receiving $20 a day plus room and board. In 1954, this was a great deal—indeed far more money than a student could earn. It was the sort of opportunity you would expect students to take advantage of for as long as the scientists would allow.

In reality the students were content for only a few hours and then became increasingly distressed. They craved stimulation of almost any kind. The scientists allowed them access to a few options, all of which were what the students would have considered boring: some gladly attended a talk on the dangers of alcohol. Others were given, and requested for repetitively, a copy of an old stock-market report. They were so bored they were ready to engage in things that they would have had no interest at all in the past. Indeed they even said they looked forward to being tested, but puzzlingly tended to find the tests tiring.

They found the whole circumstance rather difficult to take. The reward was no longer enticing enough and students started to give up the $20 a day even though they needed the money.

What these studies show is that creatures as simple as a lab rat or as complex as a human being have an internal need for novelty and discovery; and we will go to great lengths to seek it out. It is a fundamental need that requires no external motivation. We all have that inner pull.

In distinction to intrinsic motivation, motivation that can be enhanced or diminished by outside value or causes is called extrinsic motivation. These external motivations are entirely subjective to each individual. For example, a student who does his homework because he doesn't want to get in trouble is motivated by a desire for compliance or a fear of punishment; a student who works because he wants to do well in school is motivated by self-interest and working towards a goal. Intrinsic motivation is present in most individuals but external forces influence the strength of their motivation.

Extrinsic factors can also initiate initial interest in a particular pursuit—for example, starting to play tennis because of health reasons—which then develops into intrinsic motivation as the activity itself provides satisfaction. It is this transition from extrinsic to intrinsic motivation (external forces developing into internal desire) that can be very useful to us in helping students perform better in school.

How do we motivate students and learners?

Since education in schools and universities is not intrinsically interesting to most students, how do we motivate students or ourselves to value the educational endeavours? What helps augment self-directed interest or motivation and what lessens this interest?

First **positive feedback** on a competence level, such as praise for the work done or actual measurable change in performance, increases self-directed motivation whereas negative performance feedback or criticism diminishes it. **Feedback should not be personal "<u>You</u> are excellent" or "<u>You</u> are perfect" is not the best way to praise. It is better to praise the work: "You played the game really well" or "You hit all the right notes."** Both of these are praise for the work and not for the person. This feedback and sense of competence must go with a sense of independence to result in increased self-directed motivation. This sense of internal control is extremely important in fostering motivation.

Tangible rewards and threats by themselves diminish self-directed motivation partly because they are perceived as reducing independence and increasing outside control. So if motivation is **only** because of the rewards students will receive rather than a step towards independence, the extrinsic motivation will not get converted to an intrinsic one. As an example, if a student's only motivation to attend class is to receive a reward, the day that reward is removed will be the last day the student attends. Only intrinsic motivation will make him go to class without the promise of reward or punishment. In fact, it is probably even worse if the behaviour is solely shaped by fear of punishment. When that fear disappears the motivation also vanishes.

Praise is the most effective reward in engendering the development of a more intrinsic response.

I like a saying attributed to a psychologist and teacher "Praise like penicillin must not be administered haphazardly." (Ginott, H. G. (1965). Between parent and child. New York: Macmillan.) There are rules about handling medicine and there are similar rules about administering emotional medicine. In my practice as a psychiatrist you learn very quickly the potency of words. Learning how to use them is an art rather than a science but I have one golden rule: Praise or critique the action but never the person.

When critical feedback is personal, it can have a detrimental impact. "You are disgusting" is worse than saying, "You need to keep your shoes clean." Learning to give feedback that is direct but focused on actions and not the person is the key to help shape behaviour.

Feedback is not just from the outside. It is also what we tell ourselves. If we are overly critical (or, conversely, overly complementary) or if we do not perceive feedback at all then the system does not work. It is essential that we assess whether we are making progress at regular intervals. Be aware of how you are doing. Use that knowledge to course correct. If you are doing well, complement and reward your accomplishment. This spurs further progress towards your goal. Feedback, works best, when it is close in time to completion of the task.

The Art of Learning

What does this mean for us as a student? How can we use what we know about the science of motivation to help us learn?

The rapid progress of scientific understanding in this area tells us how motivation can be developed and used as a driver of our personal progress. But what we are interested in is how to use what we know to increase our ability to learn.

The key principles we can derive from the science of motivationare:

1. Motivation that is intrinsic is better than that which is driven by rewards and punishments

2. Rewards are better than punishments. Giving your-self credit and maybe a small reward can foster continued motivation. Beating one-self up can reduce motivation.

3. Negative extrinsic forces can push an individual to lose interest. A lack of control, overbearing teacher or parent, difficulty with being able to participate, unrealistic expectations or goals, or a nasty environment can diminish any and all intrinsic motivation. Negative feedback that is persistent and devaluing and constant reinforcement with rewards or by threats can lead to a state of giving up and apathy. So focus on the positive rather than negative elements. If you receive negative feedback focus that the feedback is more about performance than on you as a person. This can help refocus on the positive aspects of learning.

4. Rewards can get one started, especially if the task is of low interest to begin with. Give yourself small rewards for completing and starting something new.

5. If the task is of high interest any way, praise rather than tangible rewards keeps the fire burning and finally rewards for

achieving competence or performance also keeps up motivation. Praise your progress early and often.

6. Choice and the prospect of self-direction boost motivation by stimulating independence. So as a student, it is beneficial to try to understand first why one is studying a subject and how it could be useful later on can promote interest and direction. Teachers or parents who encourage independent thinking catalyse greater inquisitiveness, self-directed behaviour and motivation than controlling parents or teachers do. Students who are unduly controlled by outside factors (rewards and punishments) lose originality and do not think on their own as well, especially when learning is complex or require abstract, resourceful thinking.

7. Children of parents who support independent thinking do better in terms of creativity, inventiveness, resilience, and curiosity than children of parents who are controlling or micro managing. Parents and teachers who promote independence can motivate students to do the same and build and integrate this element into their sense of self and provide direction for their long-term development.

8. Intrinsic motivation combined with independence and engagement promotes better performance, fewer dropouts, and higher quality learning with greater psychological health.

9. The greater we manage to internalize our interest and desire for what we are doing, the more it becomes part of our nature and the extrinsically motivated actions now become self-determined and intrinsic.

When the independent, self-directed behaviour and motivationare integrated and assimilated with the personal development of the individual it becomes intrinsic and self-directed. Understanding motivation, its development and implementing methods, techniques and policies is necessary for successful education to take place—especially one that promotes independence creativity and critical self-directed behaviour and thinking. In the next chapter we will discuss the role of ability, benefit, confidence, and desire in starting and building motivation.

The ABCD of Motivation Ability, Benefit, Confidence and Desire

"If I were dying my last words would be: Have faith and pursue the unknown end"
—Oliver Wendell Holmes

The Art of Learning

I have a very easy way of thinking about motivation, which I call the ABCD's of motivation.

The "A" stands for ability, without ability to perform in the desired area motivation is tough to sustain. This is obvious when we think about sports, in which natural ability and physical stature are intrinsic to success in many sports; height in basketball, or bulk and strength in American football, or endurance in long distance running. Less obvious when it comes to other fields, but even here common sense suggests that some have a stronger ability for learning languages and others are better suited for math or science.

"B" stands for benefit. The individual will need to see some success or reward when they first start in a particular endeavour. If success does not come after repeated tries the individual will likely give up. The level of persistence a dogged nature becomes keys to long-term success. I will expand on this thought later in this book.

"C" stands for confidence, confidence in one's ability and confidence in achieving what one desires. The biggest impediment in trying novel and interesting activities is the lack of confidence.

"D" stands for desire, without desire there is no pull, no attraction and no drive. When starting an endeavour if there is desire it leads to a greater sense of direction, energy and maybe even a greater tolerance for failure. If there is no desire to start with and desire does not develop then motivation will diminish and vanish even with external rewards.

The Art of Learning

Our desires and our expectation of achieving those desires drive motivation and motivation as we learnt is the fuel for learning.

There are very few fantasies today that are as well-known as "The Wonderful Wizard of Oz." Written in 1900 and made into the classic film in 1939, Frank Baum's story has remained in the collective consciousness and has been highly influential in many spheres. The story is about a girl Dorothy who finds herself in a strange place after a cyclone hit her house. She is told that she has to go meet the wizard of Oz. And to meet him she has to follow the yellow brick road to the City of Emeralds. During the journey she first meets a scarecrow that wants to go with her so that he can find a brain. Then she comes across a Tin Man who wants a heart and joins her in her expedition to find the wizard of Oz. Then they come across a lion that has no courage and is afraid. He joins the group to find the Wizard and get courage. At the end of the tale when they meet the wizard they find out that he is but "a little old man, with a bald head and a wrinkled face" and a humbug.

His words to each of them are telling:

> To the Scarecrow who wants a brain: "Can't you give me brains?" asked the Scarecrow. "You don't need them. You are learning something every day. A baby has brains, but it doesn't know much. Experience is the only thing that brings knowledge, and the longer you are on earth the more experience you are sure to get."

> To the Cowardly lion who wants courage: "You have plenty of courage, I am sure," answered Oz. "All you need is confidence in yourself. There is no living thing that is not afraid when it faces danger. The True courage is in facing danger when you are afraid, and that kind of courage you have in plenty."

And to the Tin Man who wants a heart: "How about my heart?" asked the Tin Woodman. "Why, as for that," answered Oz, "I think you are wrong to want a heart. It makes most people unhappy. If you only knew it, you are in luck not to have a heart."

Its durable theme is the discord between capability and self-confidence and how the Scarecrow, the Tin Woodman, and the Cowardly Lion all lack self-confidence despite evidence to the contrary. The Scarecrow believes that he has no brains and is not intelligent, though he comes up with clever answers to several difficult challenges that they encounter on their journey. The Tin Woodman believes that he lacks a soul or heart, but is moved to emotion and indeed tears when calamity befalls the various individuals they meet. The Cowardly Lion thinks that he has no courage or mettle even though he is unswervingly valiant through their journey.

Confidence is the key to developing and maintaining the desire and motivation to learn. Psychologists use the term "self-efficacy" to describe the essence of confidence. Self-efficacy is the individual's judgement of their ability and capacity to undertake a task or challenge, in other words, their belief in their own capability. This idea has a long and rich history in psychology. Self-efficacy or self-confidence is seen as the initiator and driver of change, a predictor of effort and tenacity. This measure predicts athletic performance, sales performance, and even recovery from major health problems.

Drives
change

Persistence

Self-confidence

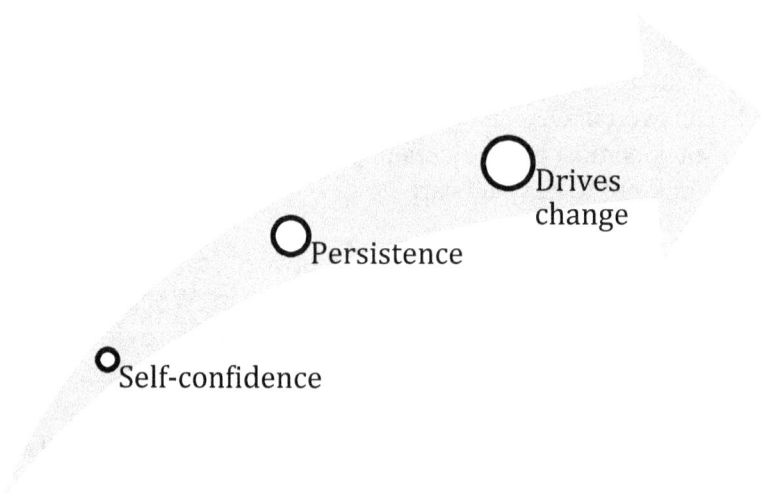

People who have low confidence in their ability to complete a task may avoid it; those who believe they are adept will join readily. Individuals, who are confident about their ability, work harder, do not give up easily and persevere longer even in the face of difficulty; those who are hesitant and lack confidence are unlikely to withstand much adversity.

We all build our internal model of who we are and what our capability is over time. Some of us are very optimistic and overestimate our ability in a given area, whereas others are less confident even when they have the ability. Our own self-esteem influences how we view our ability. Low self-esteem leads us to underestimate our ability and high self-esteem can lead to overconfidence. This sense of self-confidence in one's ability to accomplish tasks is a very important driver in building motivation.

The mental models we build of our ability to handle a given problem or task can be based on how we performed in the past on similar or related tasks, by observing others as they perform the task, and by persuasion or feedback from others. The biggest single factor is of course how well we do once we make an attempt. Success raises self-confidence and failure lowers it, but once confidence is developed, failure has less impact.

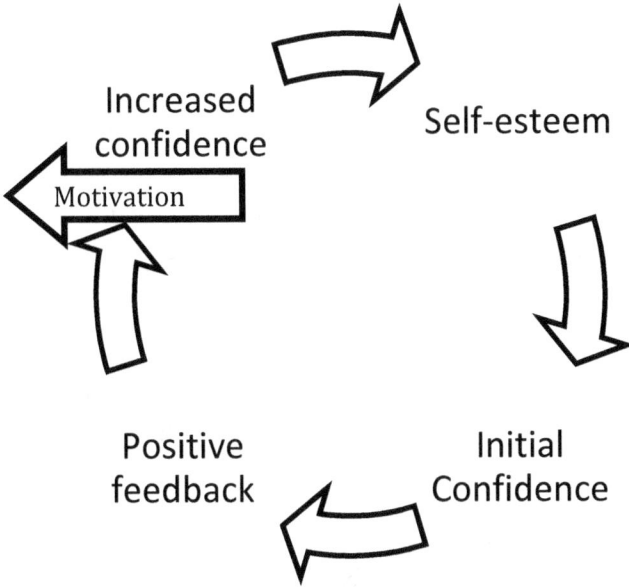

Increased
confidence

Self-esteem

Motivation

Positive
feedback

Initial
Confidence

A lack of initial confidence can be due to how we view ourselves. Some of us always expect failure or feel inadequate, despite what our actual abilities are. This attitude can become self-fulfilling. Often, people who lack initial confidence do not want to try because of a fear of failure. In this way, they will guarantee it. If you never try, you have already failed. The better and more productive choice is to ask, "Why not give it a try?" and, "What is the worst that can happen?" before you say no to attempting something new. Give yourself the opportunity to succeed. The chance of success and the resulting confidence boost aren't the only benefits. You can also improve your overall health: the propensity to gauge one's ability positively rather than negatively is a healthy predictor of wellbeing.

The second most important influence on our self-confidence is to observe others perform the same task. If we see a friend or someone else that we consider similar to us in capability performing the task then we are more likely to think we can do it too.

On the other hand, if we see that person failing we may become doubtful that we can do it. This is something we can all relate to from our own life experiences. One study had children witness a person who made either statements of confidence or pessimism while vainly struggling to crack a puzzle for a long or short time; then the children tried to solve the puzzle themselves. When they saw the person displaying high persistence and high confidence the children were motivated and persistent. When they saw the person give up even when they were sounding confident the children also felt confident. But when they saw the person behave pessimistically and without persistence the children also showed less confidence.

Similarly, when children see other children try a task and succeed, they are more likely to feel confident and try than they would be after watching a teacher or parent solve the problem. It is far more motivating to watch someone we view as similarly capable complete a difficult task than it is to watch someone we consider *more* capable. When it is someone we see as an equal, we are far more likely to say, "I could do that."

However, just seeing others undertaking the task and succeeding is less convincing than one's own performance. Let's say we see a friend succeed in learning how to swing the golf club before picking up our own club to try. If we are able to pick it up quickly then we end up feeling that we can indeed learn how to play golf. But if we have difficulty our confidence can get sapped and we may want to give up. In these instances, feedback can make all the difference.

When students are told they did just as well or better than others (or when they see someone else fail too) their confidence gets boosted. This increased confidence can lead to more perseverance in continuing to try the task.

The Art of Learning

Taping oneself and then watching for opportunities to improve can also boost confidence and performance. This tactic is familiar in the realm of sports, in which athletes watch their own and rivals' performance as a standard way to get mentally prepared and improve their game. It is uncommon in academic settings although we use this in training medical students how to examine patients.

When we want to try something new we often find friends and family cheering us on. Go to any soccer game for children and you will see parents yelling, "You can do it". This can help motivate a person to try and get started but is not enough by itself to build confidence unless the person does well when they are performing the task.

Confidence relates to how much effort is needed. Interestingly when students watch television as a vehicle for learning they report much less effort and more confidence then when they have to read material. But the learning was not any greater—in other words more confidence and less effort do not translate into more learning.

Sometimes, our own body sends signals that can affect confidence. Little signs of anxiety—our heart starts palpitating or we start sweating—can make us lose confidence in our ability to perform. A little bit of "butterflies" is good but too much and it hinders our performance.

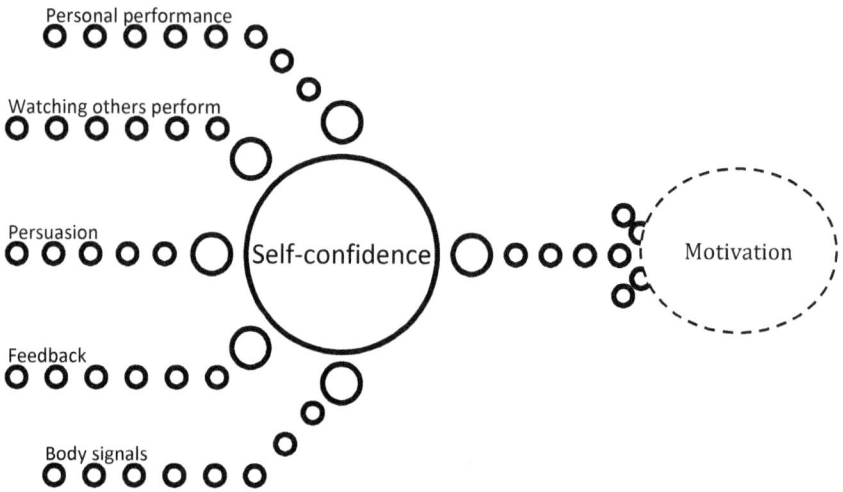

Self-confidence is an important element in promoting learning, especially academic learning. At the start of new course students are likely to feel unsure of their competence in an unfamiliar subject. They may doubt their ability to do well, obtain knowledge, develop or perform skills and master the subject. In these scenarios, our initial self-confidence will vary as a function of aptitude (e.g., skills, gifts and attitudes) and most important prior experience. Once the course starts, other factors come to operate, including one's real ability. From these elements we develop indications as to how well we are learning, which influences our self-confidence for further learning. Motivation increases when we make progress in learning and decreases when we run into problems and difficulties.

The Art of Learning

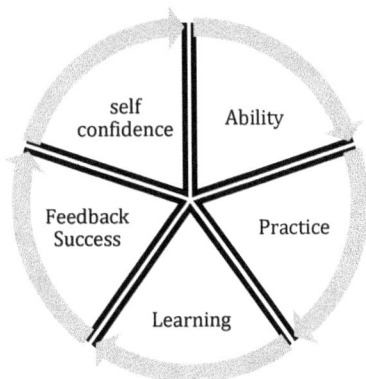

Self-confidence is usually not present for everything that one undertakes. Students can have high self-confidence in some areas, areas; say athletics, than other areas or subjects. But even within the same area, in this these case academics, they may have higher confidence in chemistry rather than mathematics. This can even vary within a single subject—students may feel more confident about physical chemistry than organic chemistry. Self-confidence is a measure that fluctuates with how much effort is needed to accomplish a task and when the task gets difficult confidence can wane.

Over time, we develop a realistic sense of our strengths and weakness as we undertake different tasks.

But confidence alone does not drive motivation and learning. There are other factors at play.

Our desires and our expectation of achieving those desires are essential. If we do not believe there is value in a particular pursuit, we are unlikely to desire to spend our energy on it. Similarly if we think it is impossible to achieve then there is no motivation to even try.

The more uncertain we are that our own actions can lead to the desired outcome the less we feel that we are in control, which in turn diminishes our motivation. This perception of being in charge of our own fate is very important. Students who are confident in their ability to learn and are in an environment where their success can be attributed to their work develop intrinsic motivation to learn and succeed. If the student feels that merit is not a factor (i.e. everyone gets good grades or everyone gets bad grades) then there is no perception of control and nothing to be gained by working hard. In this scenario, the student is likely to lose motivation and interest.

When students attribute their success to ability and hard work, it reinforces confidence and increases motivation to learn. It also builds a sense of self and self-efficacy. In other words, it builds a sense of self-worth and self-esteem that in turn influences self-confidence and motivation.

Motivation is linked to ability, implied benefit from the activity, confidence and desire. Enhancing motivation requires a foundation of clear achievable and measurable goals. Then measuring and judging the progress and making adjustments becomes the engine for maintaining interest and motivation.

The Art of Learning

In this chapter, we described the importance of confidence in
driving and sustaining motivation. But what we are interested in is
how to use what we know about confidence to increase our ability
to learn.

1. First we need confidence to build and sustain motivation to
   learn. Motivation and interest become key drivers in directing
   attention to what we want and need to learn.

2. Second, in order for confidence to be formed one needs clear
   goals.

3. Success in achieving goals becomes the fuel to maintain
   motivation.

4. Initial confidence starts with prior experience of success,
   watching others who are similar in aptitude succeed, or
   receiving encouragement that they did just as well as others. Of
   the three, prior experience is the best initiator of confidence.

5. Confidence is sustained by feedback on progress and by
   success.

6. Confidence can be sapped by failure and encouragement is the
   key to maintaining confidence.

We need to have the confidence that we will meet our learning
goals. The greater our confidence, the greater our motivation.

Self-control: organizing and regulating oneself

"He who controls others may be powerful, but he who has mastered himself is mightier still."

— Lao Tzu

The Art of Learning

To sustain learning and keep motivation alive requires persistence. Goals are certainly important in building self-confidence and driving motivation, but what makes one stick to task? Is this innate? Can we learn how to persist?

One of the classic elements for learning is the ability to organize the learning experience and regulate how learning happens. This requires intentional, thoughtful, sustained, self-directed goal-oriented behaviours. It looks like this ability can be discerned at a very early age. A simple marshmallow test can help tell how good someone will be in delaying gratification and sticking to a task.

Walter Mischel, a psychologist and professor, developed one of the most famous studies in the history of psychology: the marshmallow test. He offered 4 to 6-year-old children a choice between getting one marshmallow immediately and waiting fifteen minutes to get two marshmallows. This simple test of self-control revealed long-term implications that could impact one's professional life, personal relationships, and even their physical health.

Mischel determined that all children had the desire to eat the marshmallow right away but, with the promise of a better reward, some devised ways to prolong their desire for gratification. The children who were able to hold off on eating the marshmallow did so by distracting themselves. They closed their eyes, pretended to play, anything they could think of to take their mind off the promise of instant gratification. These children delayed their need for immediate satisfaction to get the more attractive reward.

You can tell why this is important. Everyone knows overeating is bad for you but when you see chocolate it is hard to resist. This is the classic fight between our emotions ("eat more; tastes good") versus our thought control ("it is not good for you" You will gain weight and have heart disease"). When emotions gain we give in and when a cool head prevails we resist. The more we can delay gratification the better off we are.

In our daily life, we are confronted with thousands of these decisions: should we get our reward now, or get something better later? As a student this can translate to: "Do I go out with my friends, or study now and play after I finish my homework?" Now we have more opportunities than ever to do things. Facebook, Twitter, Google, YouTube, there is a world of things that compete with our attention and their temptations are great. Short-term emotion can quickly overwhelm long-term determination.

If we are able to resist the instant gratification of distraction or procrastination, then we are more likely to keep our focus where it belongs. This is likely to make us more successful.

Self-regulation is made up of at least three processes.

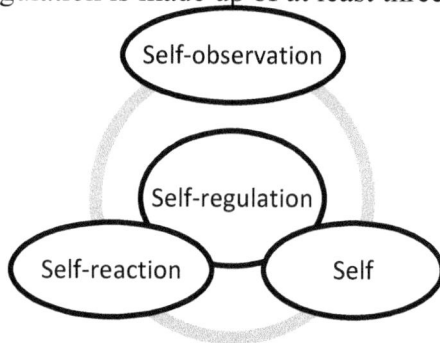

Self-observation

Self-regulation

Self-reaction

Self

The first is being aware of one's thoughts and behaviour (self-observation or self-monitoring). If you are not aware of your behaviour or actions, it is difficult to effect change. So for a student, self-monitoring will include an awareness of their actions and behaviours (i.e. how many hours are they studying? Are they paying attention in class?) If this self-observation is not systematic, or if the student regularly builds beliefs that are selective and inaccurate, their ability to change and self-regulate will be impeded. Self-monitoring has to be regular, systematic, and close in time to when the behaviour happened in order to be effective. It is so beneficial to ask yourself how you are performing, whether you are falling behind, and whether the effort that you are using is sufficient. This self-judgement monitors progression towards your goal and plays a role in confidence development and motivation. It allows you, the learner, to ask if the goal is too easy or hard and how it compares to others. And, as noted above, self-judgement reduces the illusion of knowing.

Once you have assessed your actual learning, the next step is to do something about it. *Self-reaction* is when you adjust your actions based on self-judgement. So for example, if you determine that you are falling just short of a realistic goal, you may decide to increase your efforts to accomplish it. Other times you may determine that you need outside help. It's possible that you will find that your goal is unrealistic and needs to be adjusted to fit the pace of your learning. This whole process is interactive and cyclical.

This ability to control one's impulses and work towards goals is a trait that bodes well for how well you do in life. Self-regulation operates at two levels: social emotional and cognitive (thinking) level. Both levels are in play when we learn by ourselves. Our thoughts and behaviours are directed towards achieving goals, including learning goals. This means urging oneself to put energy toward a delayed goal, rather than giving into immediate impulse.

Self-regulated and disciplined students exhibit achievement-oriented focus. They attend classes, they practice, they use learning strategies that work for them, and seek feedback.

This self-control termed by psychologists as self-regulation or self-discipline is more important than intelligence in predicting academic performance both in university students and even in middle school students. The correlation between measures of self-discipline and grade point average in studies has been twice as much as that predicted by intelligence as measured by Intelligence

Quotient (IQ). The researchers found that self-disciplined students performed better on every academic indicator from attendance to grades and performance on standardized tests. They watched less television and spent more time on homework. People who accomplish great things in life combine passion with an unwavering commitment to achieve that mission and vision.

Illusion of Knowing

Most individuals and learners cannot correctly judge what they do and don't know.

They normally overestimate how well they understand the material when they are finished studying. This "illusion of knowing" is mirrored in the assertion that many students make after they obtain a poor grade on a test:

I saw this with my students all the time: "I studied so hard. I believed I really knew the material cold. I am shocked I failed!" The problem is students often read a unit from a textbook, get to the end of the chapter, close the book, and assume they know the material. When they try to recall in class the next day, they are often chagrined to realize that they cannot remember what they read the night before

Luckily, there are ways to improve one's ability to judge what they do and do not know after studying. Testing one's knowledge is the most efficient way to overcome the illusion of knowing. Doing so will clearly show what has been learnt so that they can spend their time studying material that they have not yet nailed down.

The cue-only delayed judgment of learning procedure.

This is a mouthful but a simple way to help know one-self better.

Step One: Ask students to Allow a delay before assessing their comprehension. It is easier to recall information directly after they have learnt the material than it is once some time has elapsed. So to truly test whether one has have learnt what they have studied, it is best to wait at least an hour after studying to test their knowledge.

Step Two: Rely solely on recall—do not use cues. This is an easy way to trick yourself into thinking you know the materials better than you do. Do not allow any prompts, clues, choices, or cues when you are trying to recall information.

Step Three: Now judge how likely you are to get the answer right.

Studies done with learners of diverse ages find that when they are compelled to make their judgments after a delay and without the answer being present (e.g., viewing a question and determining if one discerns or recalls the answer without having multiple-choice answers on the same page to select from), they are very correct in their capacity to judge whether or not they know the correct answer.

This works for all kinds of material, in all kinds of languages, and will all kinds of subjects. Individuals at all age levels can define accurately what they know and what they don't know when they create their judgments in this way.

Students can use a simple rule try to remember what you read after a delay, and generate keywords or sentences that condense the main points of the chapter you just read. For instance, when individuals were asked to type the meanings for four essential terms from a text after a delay, and were then asked to appraise how well they understood what they just read, they were more able to accurately identify their level of knowledge

Thus, you break the illusion of knowing and are better able to spend your study time focusing on things you still need to learn. This leads to better performance on the final test.

Students can also use the "cue-only delayed judgment of

learning" technique when they are studying independently. Let's say a student is taking a vocabulary test that requires him to remember the definitions of 50 words. Using the technique defined above, the student should make a stack of flashcards by writing each word on one side of a card and its respective definition on the other. After studying the words and their meanings, the student should then go through the stack, looking at one word at a time and generating the meaning without looking at the other side. If the student is instantly able to generate the meaning, he can safely judge that he knows that word. If he is not sure, or if he has to peek to the other side, he should then determine if he ought to keep studying.

By objectively assessing your comprehension after studying, you are better able to allocate your time to matters that need your attention.

Mind-Set

Mind-set is a set of assumptions held by one, or by groups of people; it is a well-established mechanism that creates incentives to maintain prior beliefs, behaviours, and selections.

One kind of mind-set revolves around confidence about one's ability. Carol Dweck at Stanford talks about a mind-set belief continuum about ability and success. At one end is the belief that ability is innate, fixed, and determines success; the other end is the belief that success can come as a result of persistence, perseverance, and work on top of innate ability.

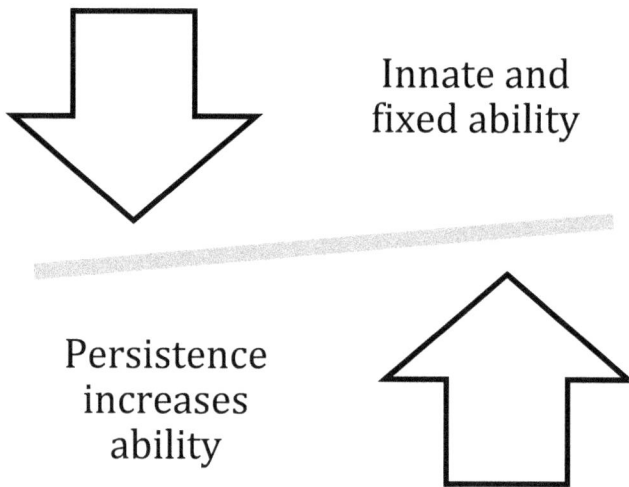

Innate and
fixed ability

Persistence
increases
ability

The mind-set she refers to is what motivates an individual to face challenges, and what can be done to develop that mind-set. Carol's view is that, "students of all ages, from early grade school through college can be taught and that their intellectual skills can be cultivated—hard work, reading, education, confronting of challenges, etc." She continues, "When they are taught this, they seem naturally to become more eager for challenges, harder working, and more able to cope with obstacles.

What does this mean for us as a student? How can we use what we know about building self-regulation to help us learn?

Learning how to self-regulate helps students stay on task and staying on task is half the battle to learn and is a critical lifelong skill. How can we use what we know to increase our ability to learn?

1. First we have to become self-aware, to be able to recognize what we are doing well and what we are not. Keeping a diary that captures what we are doing provides a systematic tool for self-awareness.
2. This allows us to judge our progress and decide how we will continue to move forward towards our goal.
3. Based on this judgement we can alter what we are doing to

make further progress towards our learning goal

4. This self-regulation can go a long way to improving learning by reducing the "illusion of knowing."

5. Just as Dweck makes the point that teaching students to value hard work and teaching then to cope with poor performance, all with the intention of putting them in charge of their own learning, we are all capable of developing intrinsic motivation and self-confidence.

The Art of Learning

Rules for Learning —A Overview of What Works

Our learning happens all the time and almost always without us ever recognizing what has happened. Learning is an innate process designed to help us learn to survive and flourish in our environment. It shapes us and makes us who we are. It leads to habits both good and bad.

So let's take stock of where we are in our learning about learning. First it is starkly apparent that learning is not a uniquely human phenomenon and the principles are consistent across species.

Learning is at its heart the intersection of attention, perception, and memory.Attention is the first step in perception and attention functions like a "spotlight" that can illuminate only a restricted quantity of material, facilitating the perception of the stimuli of interest. Attention drives perception and the perception is based on using past memory along with what is "seen" and making sense of it.

What drives attention is motivation or interest in the object of study. Motivation is apparent and essential for directed learning to occur, such as in learning to play the piano or tennis, or to study math or English literature. But you can still learn without thinking and without apparent specific motivation, such as the way in which you pick up habits.

Clearly the learning principles in general shape us but in the rest of this book I will not enter into a further elucidation of learning as the force that builds both the positive and negative elements of our personality and psychic make up. Instead my focus will be more on how to use these principles to help students learn in a way that is clearly directed and highly focused.

The Art of Learning

Rule #1 — Set Goals

Since motivation is the essential element to beginning and sustaining learning, the first set of rules will be on motivation. It begins with being clear on what it is that you want to achieve. In other words, it's about setting goals. Start with the end in mind. The key word is *mind*; visualizing and developing a concrete sense of the goal goes a long way to building motivation. All learning begins with a desire. A goal is the aim of an action that a person consciously desires to achieve. Goal setting is an important cognitive process affecting self-confidence and motivation.

Goals and the plans to achieve those goals will lay a strong foundation for your motivation for learning. Visualizing goals is, in fact, the initial path to motivation and learning. After all, how can you get started if you do not know what you want to accomplish?

If we do not develop goals consciously and for our self we risk becoming adrift and the goals are a result not of our desire but because of other causes—need for acceptance, parental desire etc. Students who set a goal or work towards a goal set by others get confidence when they hit that goal. It makes them more interested and motivated in persisting with their effort to learn. They work harder and engage more to attain the next goal. This in turn promotes a virtuous cycle.

Rule #2 — Self-Organize to Meet Goals

Building this virtuous cycle with goals, motivation, and then performance requires self-discipline and organization. Having a goal is one thing but to meet goals and develop a sustainable learning cycle requires self-regulation. It requires planning, organization, and discipline to adhere to the path of directed learning.

Rule #3 — Practice, Practice, Practice

We know this principle from the work of Ebbinghaus and we all recognize that practice is a vital part of the learning process. But we may not be fully conscious of the fact that practice is not just doing the same thing over and over, but it is focusing primarily on areas in which we are least competent and less in areas we are already proficient in.

Rule #4 — Recall What You Learnt

We have known for years that just rereading material is not as good as closing the book and then trying to remember what you learnt. Testing is a form of recall. The testing effect refers to a boost in the long-term retention of information as a result of taking a test. Think of this rule as a second step to practice.

RULE #5 — Space Your Learning

How can you use repetition to your advantage? What is the most advantageous way to space your study sessions? Classical studies suggest that the best time to re-read or repeat studying is when you have almost forgotten the subject. We will explore this in detail with specific tips on when and how to repeat.

RULE #6 — Mix It Up

In virtually every type of course or sport that we study or learn there are many topics and subtopics, be it a course on the heart or the nervous system, or English Grammar or calculus or a sport like baseball.

Most of us study by first focusing on one topic then, when we complete that topic, we go to the next. It may seem that the best way to learn multiple topics is study one thoroughly before moving to the next. The process feels natural and is one that we are all accustomed to. But this intuition is a fallacy. In fact mixing up material we learn within and across subjects enhance learning.

Rule #7 — Learn with Friends

Humans have always learned from each other and from their interaction with the world around them. We know we do if we reflect on our own experience. Children can pick up behaviours just by watching videos or cartoons and, conversely, if they see punishment for that behaviour in what they observe it reduces their inclination to imitate that behaviour.

Even as adults we learn all the time by our engagement with peers and other adults in the real world and today through our links to the cyber world. How do we work with friends to learn?

Rule #8 — Learning Works Best by Connecting to Existing Knowledge and then by Extending It

When I was in medical school more than 30 years ago, the best students and those predicted to be successful would be those individuals who accumulated the most amount of factual knowledge that they could then apply in taking care of patients. This was equally true in most other fields of study. Turn to today, now we are swamped by an ever-accumulating tsunami of information that is easily accessible but difficult to put in perspective. Information is at our fingertips but how to apply it remains distant. This has reduced the value of rote memorization of facts and increased the value of the ability to conceptualize, search, analyse, synthesize and apply knowledge.

Learning today and for the future has to move beyond memorization of facts to conceptual understanding and application in collaborative settings. It is essential to build and extend knowledge by connecting to our store in the brain.

Rule # 9 — We Learn by Living

Curiosity-based exploration drives experience-dependent learning. Learn by remaining curious, discover, experience explore the world. As we discussed, this innate force that drives our learning gets squelched if we are not careful. We have to figure out a way to keep it alive and if it fades rekindle it.

Rules for Motivation and Goal-Setting

RULE #1—Set the Right Goals in the Right Way for the Right Time Period

All learning begins with a desire.A *goal* is the aim of an action that a person consciously desires to achieve. *Goal setting* is an important cognitive process affecting self-confidence and motivation. Setting goals makes the desire concrete and visible; most importantly, it makes the goal actionable. This along with the expectation that one can reach the desired goal leads to confidence as the ignition for the learning cycle. If you set an initial goal and achieve it, you get that early confidence; then you will commit, persist, and work more and harder on furthering that goal. Once you reach that goal, your accomplishment brings about a sense of self-satisfaction, a feeling of achievement and a spur to continue.

Goals that you set for yourself are more powerful than the goals that are set for you. With that in mind, when it comes to setting learning goals for yourself, remember the ABC's of goals:

Goals should be:

- **Achievable**(You can do it),
- **Believable** (You can believe you can do it),
- **Clear and Concise**

Students who set a goal or work towards a goal set by others get confidence when they hit that goal. It makes them more interested and motivated in persisting with their effort to learn. They work harder and engage more to attain the next goal. This in turn promotes a virtuous cycle.

How Do Goals Work?

Goals work by focusing attention direct attention to accomplishing the desired outcome. As you work toward achieving that goal (and as you notice your progress) you will likely feel energized by your work and infused with a greater sense of purpose. This extra energy and sense of purpose can make you more willing to dedicate even more time and energy to pursuing your goal and therefore more likely to persist in the face of any setbacks. As you advance closer and closer to achieving your goal, your mind will also start working more strategically, devising the specific way in which you will hit your target.

The learning cycle is built through specific, measurable relevant and achievable goals. Goal-setting works. It leads to greater effort and persistence by directing attention and energy towards meeting the goal.

Specific Goals

One of the key characteristics of a well-set goal is that it is clear and concise. MBA students who established *specific* learning goals (e.g., mastering a particular subject or completing a project) later had higher GPAs and higher contentment with their MBA program than those who set a vague or long-term performance goal for the end of the academic year. Setting specific and near term goal will feel more tangible and better enable you to outline what needs to be done helps focus attention and direction. A vague goal or aspirational goal does not lead to a path that helps you think strategically about how to accomplish the goal.

Goals should be specific and clear; goals that are general do not help. Setting a goal to "Be like Michael Jordan" will never actually help someone play basketball better—it is too vague and too broad. Similarly, "Perform to the best of your ability" is a lofty goal but it has no specifics and therefore is not measurable. If there is no way to measure your progress (or even determine what accomplishing that goal will look like) you do not know how to achieve it, what it means to achieve it and when.

Specific goals are measurable and therefore you know when you achieve them. A goal that is specific, such as "Complete ten problems with no errors," is much better. Specific goals lead to better performance and learning. Let's look at a few more examples:

Poor Goal: Get as many answers right as you can
Good Goal: Finish 6 pages of problems today
Poor Goal: Try to finish as many problems as you can.
Good Goal: Complete reading chapter this week
Good Goal: Master subject and answer all questions and problems in a single chapter this week

Self-Set Goals

When students set a goal for themselves rather than be given a goal by someone else, such as teacher, they will experience a greater sense of confidence and achievement when they attain it. This confidence reinforces their commitment to continue with the course.

Schunk, an educational psychologist who has conducted pioneering experiments, ran a very simple study asking whether self-set goals are better than goals set by someone else. He studied sixth-grade students as they studied subtraction. The teacher gave some children specific goals. Others were allowed to set their own goals. A third group was not given any goals. Children who set their own goals and those who had goals assigned demonstrated greater motivation than children without goals; but children who set their own goals developed their skill better and had more confidence.

As the students work on a course of study or toward a goal they select for themselves, they are more likely to engage in activities that will lead to goal attainment—they read, practice and extend their knowledge[8]. This increased effort and persistence leads to further progress and an increase in confidence. Self-confidence is validated as students observe their progress, which conveys they are becoming skilful.

Thus, setting the right goals for you is the key to enhancing confidence and learning. If others set the goals then they have to be acceptable to the individual, the greater the acceptance the more likely the goal will be effective. Acceptance is higher if the goal is important to the individual. In other words, if the individual's desire, expectations of meeting the goal and confidence matches the goal that is given to them then they are more likely to accept the goal. Acceptance and commitment is increased when the individual sees the goal as important and valuable. If it is not, then acceptance and commitment will not be there to motivate the individual to work towards the goal.

---

[8]Schunk, D. H. (1985). Participation in goal setting: Effects on self-efficacy and skills of learning disabled children. Journal of Special Education, 19, 307-317.
  Schunk, D. H. (1990). Goal setting and self-efficacy during self-regulated learning. Educational Psychologist, 25, 71-86. This article is a great review of this topic

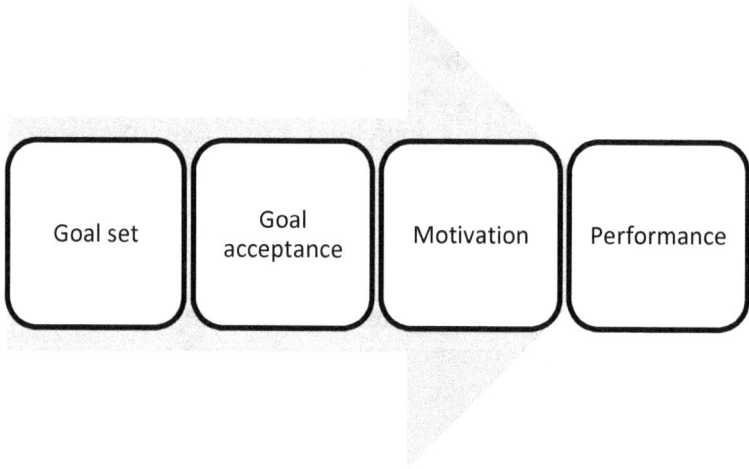

If the student feels that they can achieve the goal they are more likely to accept and commit to the goal. Self-confidence about reaching the goal and seeing it as important and valuable is necessary for the individual to accept and commit to work towards the goal.

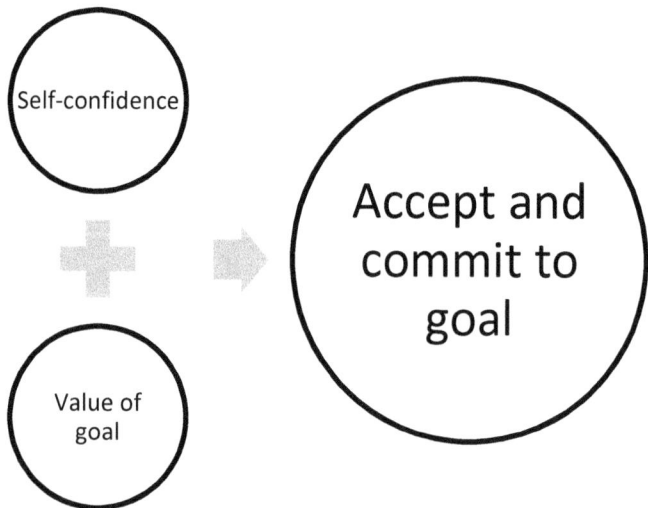

Determining Goal Difficulty

There is a linear relationship between goal difficulty, level of performance, and effort involved as long as the person is committed to the goal and has the ability to attain it. The difficulty level of goals has to be just right. If the expectation or goal is too high relative to ability or acceptance or when success is slow or not as anticipated then commitment, confidence, and interest wanes.

PERFORMANCE INCREASES UP TO A POINT
AND THEN DECREASES WITH GOAL DIFFICULTY

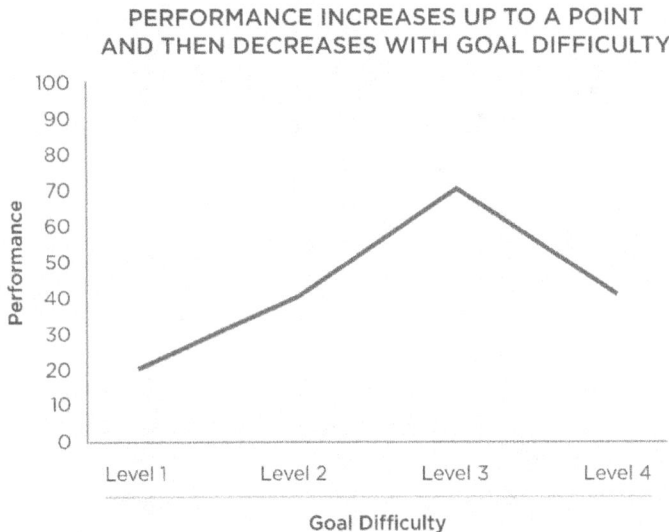

If others set the goals, then goal acceptance is very important. Indeed there is a negative relationship between goal acceptance and performance-enhancing properties of increasing difficulty of reaching a goal.[9] That is, if the externally set goal is too difficult then the acceptance is low. Assigning hard goals may not be effective when people view those goals as threatening.

---

[9]Schunk, D. H. (1983b). Goal difficulty and attainment information: Effects on children's achievement behaviors. Human Learning, 2, 107-117.

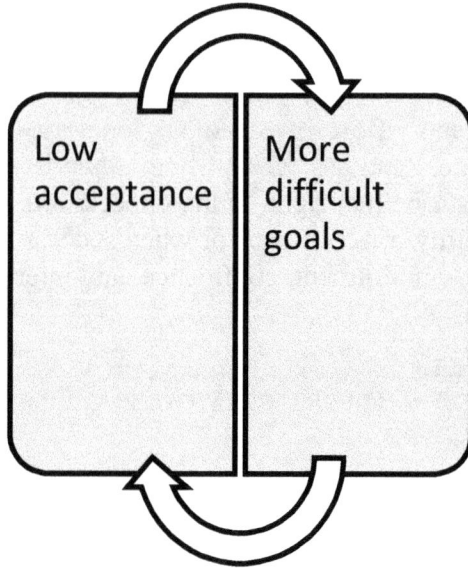

But goals should not be so easy that they are not challenging. If they are too easy they do not motivate. When one starts a new activity, goals should be realistic and at lower levels of difficulty—there is no point in thinking about climbing Mt Everest when you have never climbed before. The goals cannot be too easy either or else achieving them will not lead to a sense of accomplishment. Pursuing achievable goals increases confidence when you are starting out, but increasing the difficulty of goals as skills develop increases learning. Studies show that goals that are just beyond easy achievement increase student performance and learning. If goals are too hard there will be a tendency to shortcut the work.

So how do we get the goal right? One way to think of this is to ask, *what is the threshold level of difficulty of a goal that motivates me*? (This is commonly referred to as a *boundary goal*.) A simple way to think of this is as a motivational threshold goal (a minimum level of a target or ultimate goal). Let's you would like to score 100% on a test—that could be an aspiration goal—but you

The Art of Learning

would be satisfied if you could get 80%. If 80% were sufficient enough to motivate you to study, it would be your threshold or boundary goal. A motivational goal can be the better choice if it will actually spur you into action. When setting a goal, it is a worthwhile exercise to ask yourself what level would be acceptable to you, as this can keep you from developing unrealistic aspirational goals.

Timing of Goal Completion

Goals should not be too distant in the future. They should be in the near term. Goals that are far out in time do not easily build self-confidence since it will take a long time to achieve and you can lose interest before then.

A small study of teaching young children how to subtract, illustrates this principle.

One group of kids were told, "Try to complete as many pages of material as possible," the second group was told, "Consider setting a goal of completing at least six pages of instructional items each session," and a third group was told, "The goal should be to complete all the material about 42 pages by the seventh session." Note: the last group was not given any instructions. Instead, they were given suggestions.[10]

The children who received specific instruction to complete 6 pages during a session performed much better than the other groups. Those who received instruction that provided them a larger timeframe to complete their work did less well than the group that received the goal to complete 6 pages in a session. This group developed the most confidence and interest (motivation) and competence (skills).

---

[10]Bandura, A., & Schunk, D. H. (1981). Cultivating competence, self-efficacy, and intrinsic interest through proximal self-motivation. Journal of Personality and Social Psychology, 41, 586-598

Schunk also studied forty children as they were learning long division. They first checked to see how confident the children were that they could solve the long division problems. They all received a worked-out example and then a number of problems to solve—more than they could reasonably solve within the allocated time. They were then assigned to one of four groups. One group was told that other groups of children had solved half the problems in a session. The second group was given the suggestion that they should be able to work out at least half the problems. The third group received both sets of instruction and the final group were not given any special instructions. The children who received both sets of instructions did best and solved more problems than all the other groups. Self-confidence was increased for all three of the groups that received a specific instruction, compared to the group that received no instruction at all.

So providing both goal and comparison information about how peers performed was better than goals alone. Thus suggesting how others did, or showing how others did, can enhance the goal setting.

Goals by themselves enhanced self-confidence, while comparative information promoted motivation.

So goals that are near term, achievable with effort, and measurable drive a cycle of increasing self-confidence and motivation. Thus parents, schools and learners have to build goals that meet these objectives as a way to enhance learning. What is particularly noteworthy and striking is that goals that are set by students themselves lead to better performance than when goals are set by others.

Besides measurable achievement, immediate and direct feedback helps build confidence and motivation. You see this in sports coaching, yet it is not so common in education. It certainly should be. Formative quizzes and tests that give immediate feedback and show improvement and progress can reinforce self-confidence and drive motivation. Individual feedbacks, in addition to how we see others handling the task, are also drivers that build confidence and motivation.

Setting Goals in 4 Steps

Make the goal specific and concrete

"Study math" is not a good goal. "Solve 1 page of problems every night" is a good goal.
To better clarify your goals, ask yourself the following questions:
What is it that I want to do? Why do I need this goal? What else am I doing that can help, or may make the goal difficult?
This will help frame the goal. If the goal has many steps, make each step a sub-goal.

Make sure you have a yardstick

Be clear as to how you will measure your progress. Remember, numbers are better than words (i.e. quantitative measurement is more effective than qualitative).

Ask questions such as: *How will I know if I am on track? How can I determine where I need improvement?*

Goals need a measurement tool. For students the natural tools are the examinations that they have to take. But these tools are usually used to judge students and are not used as a way to guide and inform the students about their progress. In other words, tests are not a way to facilitate learning and motivation.
Self-testing your own ability to recall what you have learned is a very effective way of both judging how much you retained, but also a learning technique by itself. For self-testing and therefore measurement of progress timing is everything. If you are learning a

new topic, repeat self-testing with immediate feedback is best. Feedback that is delayed is not very helpful. In addition, feedback that includes the right answer is helpful so that one can learn from the errors.

- **Set a time frame** that is not too long. If it is long break it into small time increments.
- **Adjust the goal** based on how you are progressing.

If you are moving quickly, extend your goal to something more difficult. If you are struggling to move forward, scale your goal back to something easier, or add sub-goals to build yourself closer to your original goal.

RULE #2—Self-Organize to Meet Goals

Having a goal is one thing, but in order to meet goals and develop a sustainable learning cycle you must have self-discipline and organization.

Self-discipline is tied to the ability to delay desires, or willpower. Self-discipline research deals with the general question of when and how people fail to do what they should do. We see this in all areas of life. For example, we know we need to eat healthy but when we see a chocolate cake we are not able to resist having a slice; or we know we have a test to take but cannot keep our eyes and fingers from Facebook. Is this ability to delay gratification innate and fixed, or is it something that can be acquired? This question has important consequences for various parts of our life from health, to school and work. If we are stuck and cannot change or if we believe we cannot change then our success or lack of it seems preordained. Fortunately, this is not so.

Exerting self-control or discipline means making a choice respond to immediate reward or delay gratification for a longer-term benefit. This requires the ability to extinguish the stimulus to respond quickly and impulsively, and instead make a choice based on a rational basis. Nobel Prize winner Kahneman has a framework that provides guidance. He says we all have two modes of thinking. The first is fast and furious—quick, impulsive, emotional, unconscious, and hurried. The second is slow and deliberate—an analytical and consciously effortful mode of reasoning.

Fast system requires no effort; slow system requires thinking and knowledge and draws on them to arrive at explicit decisions and reasoned choices. So we have to make the slow system to be the boss. But the slow system requires energy and effort so, in addition to being more deliberate and rational, it tires easily. Too often, instead of slowing things down and analysing them, we are content to quickly take the reward rather than deliberate and make the right choice. When you want to build self-control you have to remove the emotion and quick response and go to a more deliberate practiced thinking.

So how do we learn self-discipline and slow system thinking? To learn how to delay needs a bit of planning and building a case scenario.

If-Then Method

A simple tactic for teaching self-regulation is called the "If-Then Method." In other words, if "A" happens, then you will do "B". This method is meant to develop outcome-oriented thinking, rather than reacting to our impulses.

Let's look at some examples:

"If I see a chocolate cake then I will eat no more than one slice."
"If I need to finish homework and I get a request for a Facebook chat I will delay going on Facebook until after I finish my homework."

Or let me illustrate with an interesting study with children who have attention deficit disorder:

These children have a hard time keeping their attention focused and difficulty in delaying gratification. The researchers built a simple computer game to check the ability of children to delay gratification in which children had to decide 40 times between an immediate and small (red pictures with a reward value of one point) or a delayed and big gratification (blue pictures with a reward value of three points). One group of children were told simply *red is one point and blue is three points*, the second group were instructed to get as many points as they can—they were given a goal—and the third group were given an additional if-then instruction: *Whenever a red picture appears, then wait for the blue one.*

Guess what, the group that were given the if-then instruction were able to delay gratification and performed much better on the task then the other two groups. So just having a goal was not enough; giving an explicit if-then instruction improved the ability to reach that goal.[11]

Many, many studies have shown the value of this approach. The research shows that learning slow deliberative thinking and using it to delay gratification is indeed possible. But If-Then has a limitation in that it is specific. If we try doing it in all aspects of life we cannot function and will soon be exhausted, irritable, and maybe difficult for others to work with us. But If-Then is very valuable to use if one develops the key scenarios to tackle. This brings us self-regulation.

If	Then
See chocolate cake	Think of weight and avoid
Get on Facebook	Think of finishing homework before getting on to Facebook
TV game show comes on	Record and watch after completing assignment
Friend calls you	Tell them you will call later after you finish assignment

Self-regulation is made up of at least three processes.

The first is being aware of one's thoughts and behaviour (self-observation or self-monitoring). If you are not aware of your ~~behaviour or actions, then it~~ is difficult to change them. So for a

[11]Gawrilow C, Gollwitzer P, Oettingen G : (2011)If-Then Plans Benefit Delay of Gratification Performance in Children With and Without ADHD Cogn Ther Res 35:442–455,https://www.psych.nyu.edu/gollwitzer/Gawrilow%20Gollwitzer%20Oettingen_Delay%20Paper_CoTR_2011-1.pdf

student, self-monitoring will include an awareness of their actions and behaviours (i.e. how many hours are they studying? Are they paying attention in class?) This self-observation must be on going, however. If it is not systematic or regular it may lead to building beliefs that are selective and inaccurate that may then impact the student's ability to change and self-regulate.

Self-monitoring has to be regular systematic and close in time to when the behaviour happened. The most important aspect is self-awareness and therefore self-monitoring. That means you should check to see if you are following the right behaviour—for example, are you spending the time studying, or are you procrastinating?

As you observe yourself, you will likely recognise the patterns that you employ. To do so means developing your alertness and, from there, you can begin to discern why you do the things you do and have the patterns you have. You will also see that your habits and actions are a choice.

You always have a choice—do I expand this awareness, or do I conceal, or deny it? Examples of self-observation could be of "zoning out at class" or "daydreaming or talking or checking your Facebook every few minutes while you are doing homework," or "feeling sleepy when you open your book to study." Once you are cognizant, and have deepened your alertness, you are now accountable and you have a choice as to whether to change/do things differently or not. If you mean to change your way then it may not be immediately clear what the next step is, but you have a clear goal to change. This means you can ask for help to change.

One simple way to increase your self-observation and reduce falling into the "illusion of knowing" trap is to monitor what you know but with a delay after finishing the learning session. Monitoring how you are doing right after studying may cause you to fall into the trap "illusion of knowing". Having a delay before you assess how you are doing reduces this illusion.

Study Task	→	Delay	→	Test

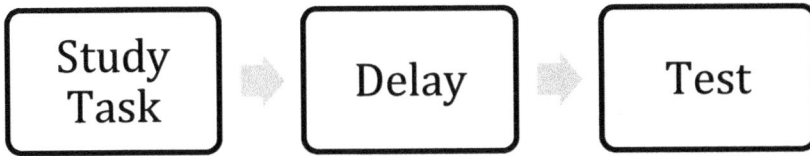

Just thinking back and saying I think I know it does not help. It is better to test yourself. You can do that by recalling everything you remember from the study session, writing it down and then going back to see if you missed something. This simple act of delaying and testing gives you self-awareness of where you are. If you are going to use cues as the way to recall, do not have the answers in the same page. By offering yourself cues, you may fool yourself into thinking that you know by seeing the answer in front of you. It can impact your self-observation.

Self-judgement is to use the self-monitoring to ask how you are performing, whether you are falling behind, whether the effort that you are using is sufficient etc.

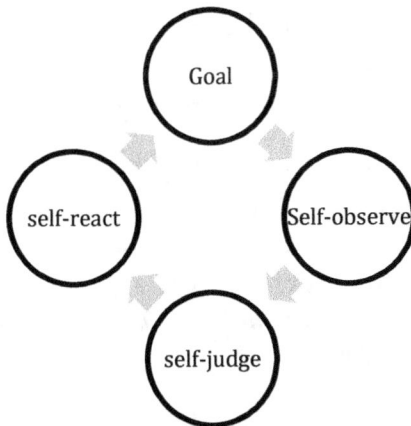

```
              Goal
             ↗    ↘
    self-react      Self-observe
             ↖    ↙
            self-judge
```

Self-judgement monitors progression towards your goal and plays a role in confidence development and motivation. It allows you, the student or learner, to ask if the goal is too easy or hard and how well you are performing compared to others.

Self-reaction is when you adjust your actions based on self-judgement. So for example, if the goal is not realistic then revising the goal. But if it is realistic, then adjust your effort to accomplish that goal.

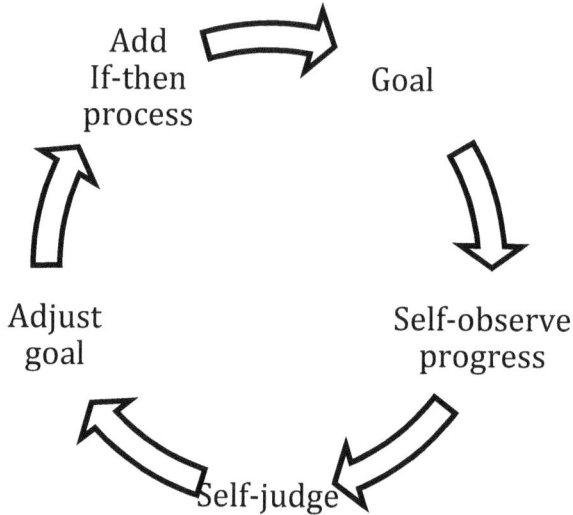

This is where the If-Then Method comes into place. If you identify where the particular situation leads to the problem then you can use an if-then scenario to reduce the problem.

As an example, if the problem is you get distracted easily when you study, you would build an If-Then scenario that says *if I am studying, then I will leave my phone somewhere else.* Or, if procrastination is the problem, then a potential If-Then scenario could be *if I am going to watch the football game, then I need to finish my homework first.*

This whole process is interactive and cyclical. This overall cycle reinforces the need for self-discipline to organize and follow through. The ability to control one's impulses and work towards goals is a trait that bodes well for how well you do in life. Self-regulation operates at two levels: social emotional and at the cognitive (thinking) level. Both levels are in play when we learn by ourselves. Our thoughts and behaviours are directed towards achieving goals, including our learning goals. This means that instead of giving in to immediate impulses, we need to focus our energy towards longer term or delayed goals.

A Few Tips to Build Self-Discipline

How many of you start out the New Year with a bunch of resolutions? How many of you follow through? How many start out the next year with a promise to do better? Building self-discipline could make the difference between accomplishing your goal and falling short again and again. Here are a few tips to build this crucial ability:

Stop coming up with excuses to delay starting

This is the biggest barrier for most people. The mind always comes up with one more reason to postpone, thinking *I will start tomorrow.*

Be honest; tell yourself why you are not starting. *I am afraid. I am bored. It is too hard.*

Just being honest gets you reasons that you can use to overcome your delay. Procrastination can become the enemy. If you struggle with delaying gratification then you have a little bit more work to do.

Come up with a goal and a plan

Everyday write down what you need to do. Look at it and see if you made any progress.

Start with the easy items. The more you cross off the list, making progress, the easier it gets. Feedback is important

Find support

If you really have trouble and you have always had trouble with self-discipline having a coach or a friend or spouse or parent pushing you along nudging you can help.

Stay away from distractions

If checking Facebook is a problem, keep it away or another measure set a designated time for you to check.

Give yourself a pat on the back whenever you hit a goal

This can keep you motivated and help move along

Just a slip should not become the start of a slippery slope. Do not use this to revert back to the same problem

Learn the scenarios that keep tripping you up. Then form a set of if-then steps to use. Make if-then the routine habit.

Self-discipline problems affect many things in life and the steps outlined above are in many ways the same as that you would follow in order to break a habit or change a compulsive behaviour. The principles are the same.

And if you cannot do it by yourself, get professional help (a counsellor, teacher, or psychologist) it may be worthwhile.

RULE #3—Repetition Rules and Practice makes perfect

Learning and motivation are extremely important if we wish to pursue and improve any field, skill, or sport. But they won't get you far without action that comes in the form of work and practice. As Pele said, "Everything is practice."

Most athletes are finely tuned machines, spending their lives trying to perfect their craft and looking to gain every physical and mental advantage possible over their opponents. They exemplify the credo that hard work leads to rewards. Just look at Tiger Woods' daily routine as posted on his web site. He starts the day with an hour of cardio-exercise and an hour and half of weight training. This is followed by 4 to 5 hours of golf and another half an hour of weight training. From the time he was a little child, he always practiced his golf game.

But even once he was the best golfer in the world, he still practiced to improve his game. When we see him play golf everything seems totally effortless—perfection, a joy to behold—hiding the enormous effort that went into the performance. He makes it look easy because he works exceptionally hard.

Michael Jordan was born in Wilmington North Carolina. From the time he was a small kid he was very competitive. He wanted to win every game that he played and his main competition was with himself. He practiced hard and tried to outdo his last performance. He had prodigious physical talent. But that was not enough—it was hard work that made him a legend.

When Jordan first joined the national Basketball association (NBA), his jump shot wasn't perfect. His outside shooting was not up to professional standards. Instead of just revelling in his strength, which was plenty, he spent his off-season practicing hundreds of jumpers a day until the jumper was just right and could "swoosh" through the hoops.

The Art of Learning

When he first joined the NBA, his defense also needed work. He studied his opponents and then practiced hard to improve his defensive. He monitored the areas in which he had weakness and worked to turn it into strength. His coach, Phil Jackson, wrote that Jordan's success wasn't his talent, but having the "humility to know he had to work constantly to be the best." His driven, competitive nature led him to practice hard so that he could be the best in the game.

We all know the saying "practice makes perfect." This is true not just in sports but also in most other fields of human endeavour. Anders Ericcson popularized the concept that practice is the main ingredient for success not talent. Many studies show that "intelligence" by itself is not a good predictor of success. The genuine development of success is the consequence of practice and repetition. There are no shortcuts. It is based on pushing oneself to do better and better. However sometimes this literature makes it sound like anyone can do it. I know of no evidence that supports that contention. Ability and capability and capacity are all important, although (as we noted earlier) not sufficient as a predictor of success. Self-discipline, which is what helps individuals push themselves to persevere, trumps intelligence and ability but still cannot predict success on its own. It is the combination of intelligence, ability, and self-discipline that leads to success.

Repetition and practice works not only for motor skills, but also for all forms of memory and learning. The classic work of Ebbinghaus described earlier demonstrates this principle.

Winston Churchill had a speech defect that made it difficult for him to pronounce the letter "s". When he went to visit a specialist he was told that practice and perseverance was the solution. Churchill took his advice to heart. He practiced and persevered. Churchill is known for his legendary practice of his speeches; the practice never showed but was evident in the extraordinary persuasive power of the speeches that he delivered. Another example of practice makes perfect.

Neuroscience shows that the brain actually changes with training. The brain is made up of neurons that are connected to each other by fibres. A sheath called myelin when they mature insulates these fibres. Using imaging one can see the tracts maturing. In a remarkable study of musicians researchers showed that the thickening of the sheath was related to how much they practiced. This change is more evident in young people. It is remarkable and compelling evidence about the power of practice.[12]

Innate talent only gets you so far. Beyond that it is hard work. Almost everyone who has achieved greatness in their fields worked hard above and beyond others. Many people believe that you need at least 10,000 hours of practice to become truly great. In his book *Outliers,* Malcolm Gladwell talks about the lives of many successful individuals and how at least part of their success was due to large amounts of practice, 10,000 hours being the golden number. He notes that the Beatles spent thousands of hours practicing and playing in Hamburg between 1960 and 1964 before returning to England with their distinctive sound. While those years were certainly not glamorous, the many hours of practice in smaller clubs and shows helped the musicians hone their craft.

---

[12](http://www.brainmusic.org/EducationalActivitiesFolder/Bengtsson_practicing2005.pdf)

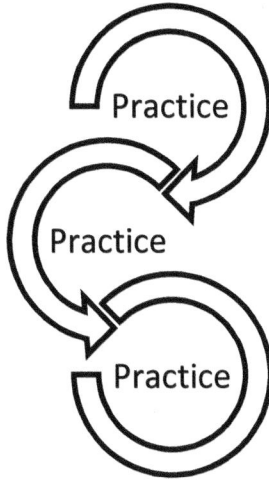

Simon and Chase said that chess masters have to play for almost ten years to attain an international level of performance in chess. They also note that these chess masters retained 50,000 patterns of regular game positions in their memory banks. Thus whether it is sports, chess, or giving speeches, repetition (and a lot of it) is the basis of excellence. To become an expert in most fields requires lots of practice and can take time, often 10 or more years.

There are many ways to incorporate repetition into your learning process:

1. Repetition. Repeat the same thing over and over until it is committed to memory. This is known as Verbatim Repetition.
2. Repeat the same information, but change the words slightly. This is known as Paraphrased Repetition.
3. Re-read the same material over and over.
4. Repeat, but add examples, demonstrations, illustrations, and other ways of providing contact.
5. Test yourself. Practice recall and see if you can write down what you studied.
6. Discuss your learning with others. Collaborate, work in a team environment, even just explaining what you are doing to another person will help you lock in the concept.

7. Repeat information with other perceptual modalities. For example, use sound instead of simply reading.
8. Repetitions can also be made through different learning media (text, audio, video, web discussion, etc.)
9. Employ memory techniques.

Some of these methods are better than others.

In general, different types of repetition are better than the same type maybe because more regions of the brain became engaged. It can also be pretty boring to make the exact same repetitions each time, which may cause our brains to tune out. Variety will keep our brains engaged and focused. But simple repetition by itself is not enough. You need to know when and how to repeat. As Vince Lombardi said, "Practice does not make perfect, perfect practice makes perfect."

RULE #3 *REFINED*: It is Not Just Simple Repetition, But Planned Thoughtful and Deliberate Practice that Counts

The relation of IQ to outstanding performance is rather weak in most domains, including music and chess. IQ is a poor predictor of success in most occupations, be it scientists, engineers, or medical doctors, the correlations between ability and occupational success accounts for less than 4% of the variance.

What is even more striking is that this relation between aptitude and ability in predicting performance decreases over time. One of the reasons could be the amount of effort and practice; the other is the nature of the practice. When we just repeat without a plan we will hit a point where there is no more improvement, a plateau. It is quite hard to overcome this plateau and to do so requires a change in approach.

What is needed is thoughtful planned practice that is designed to improve performance. This practice has two features. The first is doing more of what gives you the most trouble; the second is to determine how well you are performing and use feedback to improve your performance.

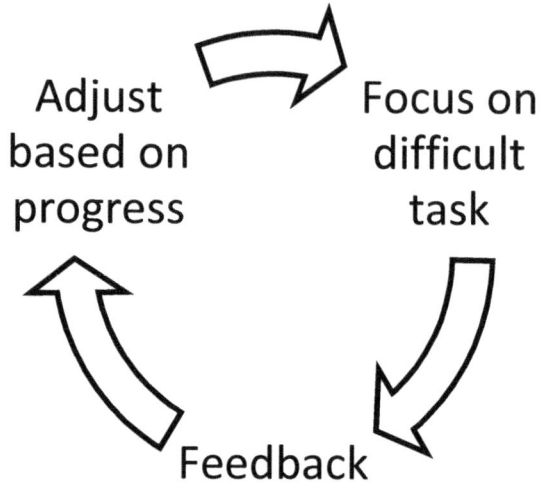

Adjust based on progress → Focus on difficult task → Feedback → (cycle)

It is not practice of what we already know but of what we do not know that well. If you are learning to play tennis and you are excellent with your backstroke but not so good with volleying then the focus of your practice should be to improve volleying. In other words the focus is not just repetition but on practicing that which is not perfect. Focus on what you need to improve while still continuing to practice what you are good at. This is the same as Michael Jordan working on his jump shot and defence till he became perfect.

The goal of deliberate practice is relentless skill enhancement, not just skill conservation. One has to not only allocate as many hours as possible but also make the best use of the number of hours dedicated to that activity. For practice to be most effective one should identify those tasks that are most likely to lead to the desired results.

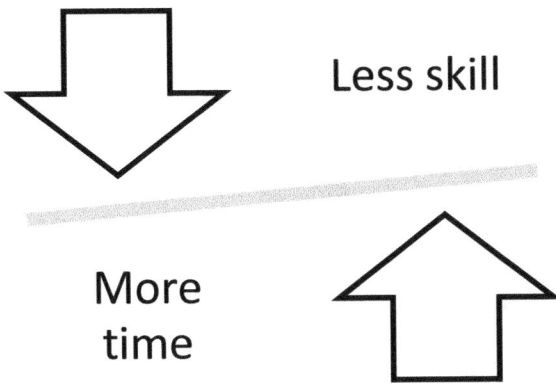

Less skill

More
time

The power of focused planned and thoughtful practice has been demonstrated not just in sports but in many other spheres, including communication, performing arts, science, and writing. The accumulation of planned and deliberate practice over time builds the skills, knowledge, and features that can lead to improved performance. In turn, it can also build a skill set that can enhance the type of training that helps continued growth and maximal performance—indeed "a virtuous learning cycle".

Human nature makes this a bit unnatural since the tendency is to focus on what you are already good at. This usually means you end up doing things you like and are good at rather than building up the areas in which you struggle. This kind of planned deliberate practice is not inherently fun or enjoyable, and therefore unless it is engaged in as a means to improve oneself or in working towards a very clear goal, there can be a rapid decrease in interest and motivation.

The Importance of Deliberate Practice

Deliberate practice is also useful in preparing for the unexpected. It is important for basic development of skills and expertise, but its true worth comes in preparing for the unexpected. In other words, practice will make you ready for those rare events that will require you to execute what you have learned, even when encountered for the first time.

Most simulator based training as when training pilots are designed not just to improve flying skills but also to make them ready for the rare circumstance by practicing those scenarios. In other words they include both a simulator to get the feel and practice of flying but also simulation of situations so as to become familiar as to what to do under those circumstances. Over 200 studies have shown that combining simulation training with regular flying training is more effective than flying alone. Thus this is the standard for training and maintaining certification for flying.

At our medical school, training is provided to build the skills and expertise from diagnosing problems to performing procedures. There are even simulators in place that can provide the experience of delivering babies. In our setting we have complete operating rooms and intensive care units for training. Full-scale simulations of events can be done repeatedly until every student has become proficient in handling those events. When coupled with periodic training and repetition, the skills and ability to handle complex situations are maintained. These systems can also be a vehicle to build teams that can work together to handle unexpected situations. Fourteen studies of medical trainees in a number of skills, including advanced cardiac life support, surgical techniques, inserting a tube into veins, and hearing heart sounds (cardiac auscultation) showed that deliberate practice with simulators enhanced performance compared to usual training techniques.

Scenario training, as in the case of fire drills and emergency safety procedures, are another form of deliberate practice. Case studies can also be used as a forum or vehicle to learn about how to handle a range of circumstances. The case study is a very typical scenario-based method of study in medicine and now a popular method in many business schools. In all instances, these methods are developed to practice by repetition just the same as Michael Jordan practicing his jump shot.

But I do not fully subscribe to the notion that deliberate practice alone can make you an expert. Innate ability and maybe other factors that we do not know much about are equally important. A recent study by Macnamara shows that deliberate practice is important but is not the only ingredient for success. They say (and I agree), "Regardless of domain, a large amount of variance in performance is not explained by deliberate practice and is potentially explainable by other factors." On the basis of a survey of chess players, there is robust evidence that copious deliberate practice is necessary (but not sufficient). Other factors play a role including intelligence and age at which they started to learn. Deliberate practice is the only way to improve learning—but you should not think that it is enough to make you a star.

The two key tips to remember are:

1. **If you are struggling with something, or do not know it as well, practice it more.**
2.
3. **If learning through simulation is an option, use that approach as much as possible.**

In *Make It Stick,* author Peter C. Brown tells us, "The act of retrieving learning from memory has two profound benefits. One, it tells you what you know and don't know, and therefore where to focus further study to improve the areas where you're weak. Two, recalling what you have learned causes your brain to reconsolidate the memory, which strengthens its connections to what you already know and makes it easier for you to recall in the future."

In other words, practicing memory recall will give you feedback on what you might not know well, and it will further strengthen your memory of the things you do know. This brings us to our next rule.

RULE #4—Practice Retrieval of what you Learnt

In *Make It Stick,* author Peter C. Brown tells us, "The act of retrieving learning from memory has two profound benefits. One, it tells you what you know and don't know, and therefore where to focus further study to improve the areas where you're weak. Two, recalling what you have learned causes your brain to reconsolidate the memory, which strengthens its connections to what you already know and makes it easier for you to recall in the future."

In other words, practicing memory recall will give you feedback on what you might not know well, and it will further strengthen your memory of the things you do know. This brings us to our next rule.

Just as practice will help you improve a physical skill or talent, practicing memory recall in the form of self-testing will help you improve your retention and, by extension, your learning.

Ebbinghaus, the psychologist who avidly studied self-testing, showed that *recall* makes us retain information better. We have known for years that just rereading material is not as good as closing the book or iPad and then trying to remember what you learnt. The testing effect refers to a boost in the long-term retention of information as a result of taking a test. The whole flash card system that we use for learning is based on recall. Recall can be with or without a cue.

You might have used flashcards in elementary school: 5*6 =? on one side of the card, 30 on the other; or in high school Chemistry: Pb= ? on one side and "Lead" on the other; or in medical school, "Signs of cardiac failure" on one side and "Fluid retention" on the other side. This approach is tedious but effective. It requires the individual to generate the answer rather than choose one from multiple choices. A multiple choice question can be answered by a process of eliminating answers and by using clues even if one does not know the answer. The process of generating an answer from the fund of knowledge that one knows is a more powerful method of learning than just rereading material. Many early studies show that retrieving information after studying was more effective than studying once or even studying the material multiple times.

Try this for yourself. Make a list of pairs of words and memorize them by reading:

Cat — Fat

Mad — Angry

Leaf — Greens

Dad — Pop

Fad — Bad

Then test with a cue:

Cat — F

Mad — An

Leaf — Gr

Dad — P

Fad — B

Now for the same list, if you try to learn by generating the paired word with a cue rather than just reading it you will remember better. That is, given the pair Mad-An____ you generate the word "angry." The cue allows you to remember the pair better.

You can apply this principle immediately from learning words in a foreign language to math or chemistry formulas. Let's say you learn a list of English to French words. Your recall cue can work either way (i.e. give the English word and ask for French, or the other way around). Both methods can enhance memory.

This effect, in which learning is improved by testing and or generating information rather than by reading, is the *generation effect*, also known as the *testing effect* or *recall effect*. In this way, tests are not a means to learn, but rather a tool to assess a student's knowledge. The testing effect has been shown using word lists or picture lists as subject materials and also with school material.

The Art of Learning

A classic study involved college students learning a passage about a specific subject. One group read the material twice; the other read and recalled the material. When tested five minutes later the subjects who restudied did better, but one day out and a week later the students who read and recalled did much better.[13] This indicates that retesting and recalling improve long-term retention of the information.

Try this learn common phrases in a language, in this case Tamil:

Try reading four times versus "read, recall, read, and recall."

Greetings:
Vaazhthu

How Are You?
Nalamaa?

Good wishes,
-Vanakkam,

Come-:
Vaanga!

Morning!
Kaalai

---

[13](Roediger, H. L.; Karpicke, J. D. (1 March 2006). "Test-Enhanced Learning: Taking Memory Tests Improves Long-Term Retention". *Psychological Science* **17** (3): 249–255)

Evening!:
Maalai

Thanks
Nandri

You?
Nienga?

Do you notice a difference in your ability to recall the words through these two different methods?

Karpicke Study

Question: Whether using the retrieval practice studying system—(students alternate between reading a passage and writing memorable information from that passage)—improves student learning of a science passage compared to the more common "study once" method and the "study then repeat study" method, or concept–mapping techniques.
Subjects: Eighty undergraduates at Purdue University

Methods: Four groups study once, repeat study, concept mapping and retrieval practice.

Study-once: Students studied passage for a five-minute reading period.

Repeated-study group: Students read the text thrice during three additional five-minute sessions, with one-minute breaks between sessions.

Concept mapping: Students spent 25 minutes after the five-minute reading period writing the text's main concepts on a sheet of paper.

Retrieval-practice: Students spent 10 minutes after the initial reading period entering any information they remembered from the text in a response box on a computer screen. The students then reread the text for another five minutes and then again listed the information they remembered.

Science passage: All study participants began by reading a 276-wordpassage on sea otters for five minutes.

Test: One week after the experiment, participants were given a test with factual and conceptual questions about the passage.

What Did the Study Find?

Students using retrieval practice performed much better than students who studied one or those who used the study- repeat-technique. 67% average correct answer for retrieval practice, 27% for study once, 49%for repeated study, and 45% for concept mapping.[14]

It is very easy to apply the Karpicke study to our own learning. Read a passage that is not too long, maybe a page or more or a passage from a SAT reading test. Then close the material and try to recall.

Try it out:

1. Read a passage on the subject you are studying
2. Recall the key messages on the subject or take a quiz
3. Repeat
4. The more you repeat, the better the long term retention

---

[14]Karpicke, J. D., & Blunt, J. R. (2011). Retrieval practice produces more learning than elaborative studying with concept mapping. *Science, 331,* 772–775.

The benefits of testing after learning are most noticeable for test items that were answered correctly and less so when the answers were incorrect. However, to get the most benefit from testing or recalling information, the trials must have some retrieval success. If the test trials are so hard that no items are recalled, and if there is no feedback given, then learning will not occur (or may only occur minimally).

Why does testing or recall provide such a benefit over simply repeated studying?

There are two reasons: first, when we try to recall test or generate answers we form new, more profuse, durable connections between pieces of information as opposed to simply restudying (which is using the same connections over and over). Second, when we encode links between items, we are also encoding the process to retrieve those items; and testing provides practice in triggering these retrievals whereas studying does not.

Building flash cards

 We can easily build flash card to study and we can also buy pre-set flash cards for numerous subjects from language to math and science. Flashcards use the mental process of active recall: given a question, one recreates the answer. Repetition improves the recall.

The student can design their own flash cards using many kinds of free software that test information. One card may have a question and a linked answer (including for languages pronunciation using audio, images or both). Most are easy to use uncluttered piece of software, and customisable. Examples of easy to use free software, which are customisable such as:

ANKI http://ankisrs.net/

Mnemosyne: http://mnemosyne-proj.org/process.

Supermemo: http://www.supermemo.com/

Cram: http://www.cram.com/

Some, including Cram, have a range of cards on a variety of subjects. Most of the free software allows use and development of mobile flashcards for your Android, iPhone or Windows device, allowing you to take your flashcards to study when you want and where you want on the go!

Study on the plane, boat, bus, restaurant, subway or train, or when you are bored and you have some open time. When you create flashcards with these types of software and you have mobility use through your phones, tablets, and computers. They travel with you! Constantly reviewing your flash cards will guarantee you'll retain more of the information you're learning with little additional effort required. The key is making this a habit.

It is easy to be distracted by other things rather than reviewing material but making reviewing a habit can make a big difference. Our concept of seeing testing as just an assessment tool belies the potential for testing to be a learning tool. While schools and colleges may take awhile to adopt and adapt there is a potential for students and learners to use this approach to enhance learning. Besides the tools mentioned there are a number of new ventures that are using testing as learning often with games to make learning fun and resilient.

A next generation venture for test-based learning is seen at Digital-Tutors.

Digital Tutors

The Art of Learning

The site is designed to train individuals on game development and software application. The entire set of modules is designed to train individuals by testing and immediate feedback. They teach students how to make movies, games, digital art and more.

Another exciting venture is **Kahoot.** Kahoot uses games that consist of multiple-choice questions—quiz, test or exam—in any topic. The game and questions are projected at the on a screen in a classroom, and then the children play together in real-time. This interactive format is an attempt to combine games, tests, and peer learning to enhance learning and growth in young children.

Knowledge Guru is an innovative method to training that combines the power of games with learning science to maximize knowledge retention. Through an attractive game play practise connected to the rules of spaced learning and repetition with feedback. Repetition united with spaced assessment and play is used to build long-term retention.

The Art of Learning and Memory

A: Mnemonics tools to remember facts. Words, rhymes, or a phrase

B: Remember by linking (associate what you need to remember with what you know especially if it is memorable, ridiculous or funny

C: Using a hook or peg to connect numbers to memory

For learning to occur, memory is essential. Without memory there is no learning. Even though in today's world we do not need to use memory to the same extent as our forebears did, a good memory remains very valuable, and for a student it is essential since many examinations and tests still rely on memorization. We are always impressed when people remember us, not just our names but our background history and events. I have had colleagues who can remember people even if they met them just once; they remember their names, their spouse's names, where they are from and snippets of the conversations they shared in the past. This always cements relationships, makes people feel special, and leads to a reciprocal admiration and engagement.

Our interest in memory is shown by the popularity of "Memory" books. Many of these books just like diet books top bestseller lists. Memory depends on perception and observation. Perception depends on attention. Every moment of our life there are events happening and we rarely pay attention and indeed have no memory of them. If one were to ask a simple question: "How many floors are in the building that you just went to?" You may find you have difficulty providing an answer. Unless you went to the top floor I would venture to guess you would not know.

In fact, most of the time we do not perceive and observe what goes on around us, because the sights and sounds do not engage our interest. Remembering requires using attention and perception and then building association.

Association, meaning connecting things, is the way in which we can learn to remember. Anything we want to remember is better when it is linked to what we already know. We use VIBGYOR to remember the colours of the rainbow: Violet, indigo, blue, green, yellow, orange and red; or "Every good boy does fine" to remember the progression of musical notes. These are known as *mnemonic devices*.

Mnemonics, named after the Greek goddess Mnemosyne, refer to memory tricks or systems to remember. In ancient times, memorization was the only way to convey key information to others and was very critical even for their survival. As we know today, memory can also be crucial to our learning and performance in everything from educational to professional to social spheres.

One of the more popular authors in the genre of memory books is Harry Lorayne. Harry is an entertainer with a prodigious memory who has written many bestselling books on improving memory. When I was in high school I came across one of his books. I found it engaging and applied many of the principles that he described to help me learn. In those days most of the examinations in many subjects, history, geography and biology was based on regurgitating information and having a systematic approach to memorization was indeed helpful.

Besides simple mnemonic devices, one of the common techniques used to remember a list is called the "link" or "chain" method. This method is usually taught in most books on memory systems. The memory method is based on linking objects one to another. The more imaginative, visual, active and bizarre the linkage the better and easier is to remember.

The Art of Learning

Say the following sequence—car, refrigerator, cat, chair, and knife—is the order to remember. One would think of a car dragging a giant fridge, while a cat eats all the food inside, then sitting down on a chair with its legs crossed, and then a knife slicing the chair. This allows a sequential remembrance and is more effective than when trying to remember without the technique. The link technique works even with a large number of objects but it has limitations. First, it only works in sequence. It does not make it easy for you to say which object was the third in the middle. Second, forgetting one object in the sequence can throw off the rest of the list; and, third, if the same object is in the list more than once it can be confusing.

A variation of this is the "journey" method. In this method objects are linked to a specific trip where different spots on the trip can link to objects in sequence.

Here's an example: "open the door" links to object one; "get into car" to object two; "end of street" to object 3 etc. Another variant is the "room" method. This method has been in use since the roman times. It functions by imagining a room (e.g. your sitting room or bedroom). Within that room are objects. The technique works by associating images with those object objects in a room like chairs, sofas, paintings, tables etc. To remember associate what you need to recall with objects in the rooms and then, take a tour around the room in your imagination, visualising the known objects and their associated information. This technique has also been used to learn languages by using entire towns or cities and their objects and connecting the English language words to the foreign language words.

The second technique is called the "peg" or "hook" system. There are many ways to peg, the most common of which is to associate a vowel's phonetic sound with each number and use the vowels to develop objects that can be used to link the number to the new object. This requires a list of vowels linked to numbers. The

126

problem with this system is that you have to memorize the system and use it all the time to keep it current and available for use.

One of the most common is as follows:

1 is linked to vowel T or D (T has one down stroke)
2 is linked to N (Two down strokes)
3 is linked to M (Three down strokes)
4 is linked to R
5 is linked to L
6 is linked to J,,Sh, or soft G
7 is linked to K, C or G
8 is F or V
9 is P or B
0 is S or Z

To remember a list of numbers would be to make word with vowels connecting the letters so 71 could be cat or 91 is Pot

Using this system, any long list of numbers can be stored: Once you can describe objects that can be easily visualized it is easy to associate them together and form strings using the link method. The method can also be used to link a specific number to a word. This is done by making a visual object associate with each number and then uses it to associate with the list. For example 1 can be tie, 2 can be Noah, three can be mow, four rye, five law, six shoe, 7 cow, 8 ivy, 9 bee, 10 toes, and o zoo. Then when a numbered list has to be remembered these objects are connected to form the number series.

Another hook system uses shapes for numbers instead of phonetic sounds:

1 is a candlestick; 2 is Swan, which looks like the number 2; 3 is a three leaf clover; 4 is a chair; 5 is a star, and so on. The association is then between these shapes representing numbers and the

numbered items on the list, obviously these techniques are less useful in everyday life. The key to memory effectiveness is structure.

Most of the time, students have to remember short list of content sometimes in sequence and sometimes by a specific number—for example the periodic table. Although this kind of information has almost no value in the real world, especially when that information is readily available, it is still tested in exams. The link system and the simple peg numbering system either phonetic peg or space peg system will generally suffice. For language the Roman room system can be useful.

For longer lists or disparate information that has to be recalled, the journey system can help, remembering key facts at each stop in the journey. By using these simple memory recall techniques, retrieving all the facts necessary to answer an exam question becomes as simple as running through the list in your mind, jotting down the retrieved facts that are relevant to the question.

But for most of us the technique has value in our daily and work life, such as in remembering names (one of the more difficult tasks to do as one gets older). This can be helped by asking the individual to repeat their name and also by using some features of their name to remember them by. Maybe associate their name to an occupation as in the case of remembering a name like shoemaker or Schumacher, or connecting to famous person or event. Once a construct to remember is built for the name, the key is to associate it with a facial feature such as the nose, eyes, or a mole; this process requires a little bit of effort but will certainly help you put the name to the face in memory for a long time. Over the years I have met colleagues who are exceptional in doing this. They impress everyone but, more importantly, they make the individual feel special and this helps build and sustain relationships.

Imagery a Tool for Learning

In the beginning, the world is what we see with our senses. Words convey and distil that world when we speak write or read. Imagery is like creating a painting out of words. We remember better when we can visualize a scene in our mind's eye. Words that evoke images are recalled easier than those that do not. The mental models that are built by words can be not only visual representations but also could be through any of our senses hearing, smell, taste or touch. When we read about the aroma of coffee, it brings to our consciousness the smell of coffee, or we salivate when we read about the warm buttery croissants. Evoking sensations makes the material memorable.

So how can imagery help us learn better?

An experiment asked two groups of students to read a text on the nature of water and its character. One group was told to visualize the material, the other to just read the material. When tested to see if they could understand and draw inferences from the material, the group that was asked to create clear mental models performed much better than those who were instructed to just read. The effect was impressive since the instruction was minimal and there was no training to teach the students how to visualize. The study makes sense. To imagine is to make the effort to understand and organize the content and connect to pre-existing knowledge.

Effort understanding organization and connection to existing knowledge are all expected to improve learning and they do. However, imagery does not always work. Imagery works only when the text or material can be built into a visual model and the material is short and concise. It gets harder when the matter is long, elaborate and complex or if it cannot be visualized.

Imagery does not appeal to all students. Some find it easier to imagine than others. So teaching students to use imagery, works only if the student follows the instructions. In many studies when students were instructed to use imagery only some did and only those that did showed benefit. Successful students weave imagery right through the learning process.

In almost all the studies that have been conducted with imagery, the material has been friendly and easy for the student to build images. When the material is abstract and difficult to visualize, the technique does not work. Studies that compared imagery to reading showed no benefit for imagery when the passage was not easy to visualize. It works best for short, easy to visualize content and less so for complex, abstract content.

A Few Tips for Using Imagery in Learning

1. Imagery and visualization makes recall better (and easier).
2. To visualize means to attend, comprehend, organize, and connect material to pre-existing knowledge.
3. Imagery works best for short, clear, imaginable material.
4. Hearing makes seeing (visualizing) easier.

Now, let's return to repetition. Besides repeating what you do not know so well either by rereading or by recall or by testing, the question is *when and how often do you repeat*? The "how often" is clear: the more the better. All learning—whether it is motor perceptual skills, facts to be recalled or remembered, or thinking skills for the long term—is better when the repetition of the to-be-learned information is distributed over time as opposed to being repeated (crammed) in a very short amount of time. This brings us to our next rule.

RULE # 5—Space Your Learning

Cramming for an examination is very typical. This type of repetition, called "massed practice or repetition" by psychologists, is not very effective for long-term learning. If two pieces of information are learnt for the same length of time but spread over either a very short interval (cramming) or over a longer time interval, they are remembered quite differently. In other words, the sum of learning does not equate to how long we remember. Unfortunately, this is how most students study.

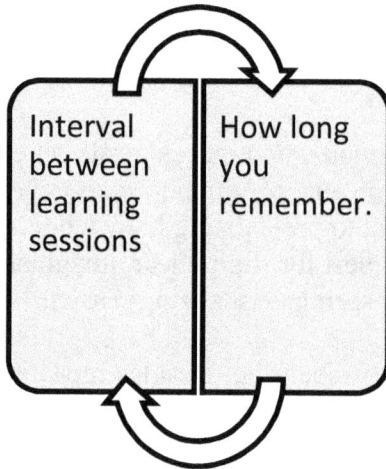

Spacing effects are seen across multiple domains (e.g., visual motor skills, perceptual learning, simple motor tasks or learning lists of words or concepts), across species (e.g., rats, pigeons, and humans), across age groups and even individuals with different memory impairments, and across retention intervals of seconds to months. In general learning, where you learn with long intervals between sessions, you remember for a longer time; but with cramming you only remember for a short time. As an example, let's take two kids: Sam and Sally. If Sally studies half an hour every day for two weeks and Sam studies the same subjects for 12 hours all on one day, the learning retention for the long term will be better for Sally than for Sam. This effect is large and reproducible.

Spacing repetitions over time facilitates long-term remembering. So instead of cramming, if we study the same material spaced over time we will remember for a longer time. Just think, if we decide we are going to play in a tennis tournament tomorrow, yet we have never picked up a racket in our life, do you think one night of intense practice will make it possible for us to play well? We would not even think to do anything like that. On the other hand, when learning is distributed over a longer period of time the learning sticks. If we were practicing tennis every day for months we would be more likely to be able to play better in a tournament.

This concept of spaced repetition is not new. Prof. C. A. Mace[15] first advanced it in the book Psychology of Study in 1932 and, at the time, the concept was not well received. Over time, however, it has come to be generally accepted.

The other principle that leads to the development of spaced learning is Jost's Law, which states, "if two associations are of equal strength but of different age, the older memory will take a longer time to decay and a new repetition has a greater value for the older memory trace." This has been around since the 1800's. The law implies that a memory that has been around longer maybe better consolidated (probably by a different brain mechanism) and that mechanism takes a longer time to decay whereas a more recently learnt memory has not been consolidated and therefore decays faster.

---

15 Mace, C.A. (1969). *The Psychology of Study.* Penguin

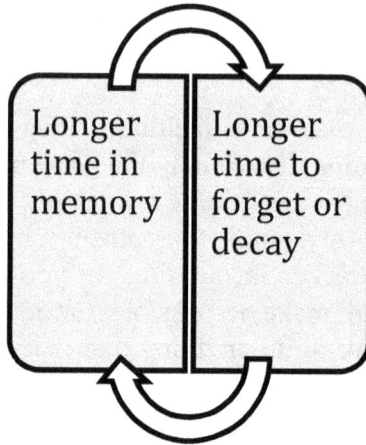

| Longer time in memory | Longer time to forget or decay |

Ebbinghaus found that memory that was present a day after learning took a longer time to decay. The other element of the law implies that consolidated memory that has been around longer is easier to strengthen by repetition, implying that less repetition is needed for already consolidated memory.

One of the early attempts to study whether having spaced intervals of time between learning is useful in the real world was by Spitzer in 1939. He used a form of expanded retrieval— increasing the time interval between tests—to assess the ability of sixth graders to learn science knowledge. Spitzer tested the entire sixth-grade population of 91 elementary schools, about 3600 students in Iowa. The students read two articles, one on peanuts and the other on bamboo, and then they were given a 25-item multiple choice test to assess their knowledge (questions such as, "To which family of plants does bamboo belong?"). Spitzer tested a total of nine groups, manipulating both the timing of the test (administered immediately or after various delays) and the number of identical tests students received (one to three). Spitzer did not incorporate massed or equal interval retrieval conditions.

The results were impressive. He found that the longer the interval between learning sessions, longer the material was retained by the students. Spitzer concluded that, "examinations are learning devices and should not be considered only as tools for measuring achievement of pupils."

Landauer and Bjork (1978) explored the result of breaks that increase over time (expanded retrieval) in two well-controlled experiments. In their study, subjects were presented a deck of cards with fictitious names, in the trials, subjects were first presented both the first and second names intact followed at varying schedules of receiving cards with only the first name of the study pair as a cue to retrieve the second name.

For example, in an expanded retrieval schedule, subjects received the first name as a cue at 1, 4, and 10 intervening cards, or at equal intervals of 5, 5, and 5 intervening cards. A massed condition (same as cramming) was used to obtain a reference point estimate of the influence of simple repetition without any interval spacing between them. The results of a recall test when they were given one name and asked to remember the corresponding name after the initial learning phase showed that having either increasing or equal intervals of time between cues (tests) that tested recall increased the ability to remember compared to those who crammed (massed condition). There was also a small benefit for the expanded interval over the equal interval condition.

Testing recall of names

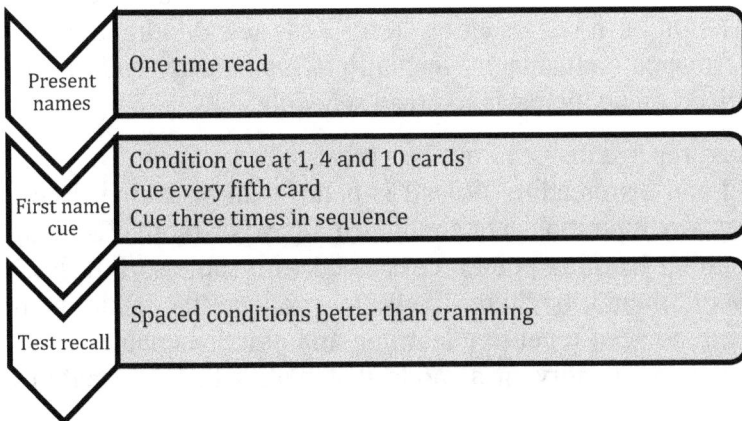

Present names — One time read

First name cue — Condition cue at 1, 4 and 10 cards / cue every fifth card / Cue three times in sequence

Test recall — Spaced conditions better than cramming

In another simple study, subjects studied a list of unfamiliar facts; they then studied them again after an interlude varying between 20 minutes and 105 days. Then, 7 to 350 days after the second study session, they were tested on their recall of the material. When tested on the 7th day, their performance was obviously better than the test on the 350th day. But retention was best if more time had elapsed between the two study sessions.

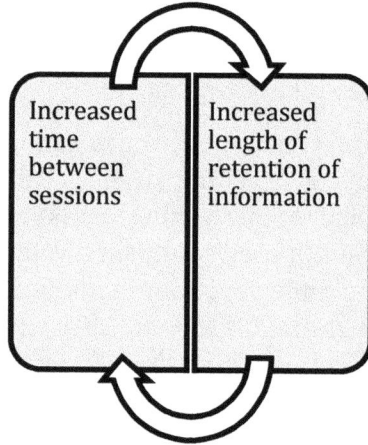

| Increased time between sessions | Increased length of retention of information |

Rea and Modigliani (1985) tested the success of expanded retrieval in a real world third-grade classroom setting. Students were given novel multiplication problems or spelling words to learn. The word or the math problem was offered together as massed spacing (cramming) or at a progressively increasing intervals of 0-1-2-4, in which they were being tested on old items and then learning new items. On a final retention test, Rea and Modigliani found a performance advantage for all items—math and spelling—practiced on an increasing spread schedule.

Spaced repetitions need not be verbatim repetitions. They could be recall and or rereading. Recall is better than rereading. Regardless of the way repetitions are conducted, if two or more elucidations of the similar learning point are repeated with some sort of time delay between them, they are likely to produce the benefits of the spacing. Spaced repetitive learning and practice enables us to store material in memory in a mode that makes the information more impervious to forgetting than non-spaced repetitions. Repetitions are good, but spaced repetitions are better.

One critical point to consider is that spacing may not produce an effect unless more than one or two or three repetitions are used. This is especially critical when difficult, lengthy, or technical learning materials are used. Let's face it: when there is a lot to learn, or when the learning material is complex, learners will need more repetitions. When learning events are spaced out, the difficulty of learning complex or lengthy materials may be compounded; and so, the advantages of spacing may only become evident when enough repetitions are used to enable a basic threshold of learning.

But spacing between reiterations is not always better than non-spaced repetitions in creating short-term memory retrieval. If the interval is very large between learning and testing, we will do less well; that is, we will remember better if the learning transpired just before testing. Learning before an exam will help you at the time of the test.

The research on expanded spacing is still a bit uncertain. Both types of spacing's—equal or expanding—are superior to no spacing's at all. In other words, it is clear that the spacing effect works whether it is equal or expanded in nature. What is unclear is determining when one type of spacing is better. If you combine what we discussed about deliberate practice then an expanded practice approach is viable—that is, the better you learn the more you can expand the interval between learning sessions. We need to refresh just as we are beginning to forget. This fits with a deliberate practice schedule.

For just reading, consistent and expanded spacing's are equally beneficial. For retrieval practice, the expanded spacing approach produces additional benefits only when we don't receive feedback on our retrieval accuracy. So when we practice, we need to check if what we are recalling is accurate. This "re-learning" effect can apply equally to spacing or non-spacing situations. A thread of research proposes that spaced retrieval practice generates learning when there is failure to retrieve. When we fail to recall, remember, or retrieve information from memory that failure can serve as a warning. Subsequent chances to learn material related to the previous failure generate more energetic and constructive learning behaviour.

Most failures to recall occur when we can't remember information—it is rarely a case of remembering the wrong information. But failure can motivate us to employ more robust and better encoding strategies when we get a later chance to learn the same information. In other words, failures generate better learning behaviour when further chances are presented. This is not better learning in general, but better learning related to the specific information we failed to recall.

Thus, spaced repetition is indeed effective and there is some suggestion that graduated or expanded intervals could be useful. Spacing repetitions over time reduces the number of repetitions that are needed to produce the same level of learning results. For example, in one experiment, the number of repetitions needed was reduced by half—simply by increasing the spacing interval between repetitions. The spacing effect is seen in a wide range of learning situations, illustrating its general applicability. It has been found in many highly controlled list-learning experiments and in classroom situations, in learning vocabulary in a foreign language, and in multimedia. Similarly, the spacing effect is seen not just in young adults, but also with the elderly and even in pre-school.

Performances on examinations that are recall based are in essence memory tests and not test of understanding. Many studies show that we will remember better if what we are tested on is exactly what we learnt. If on the other hand the test is not of the exact same content and depends on contextual use of what was learnt then the performance is not so good.

During cramming, there is relatively little chance for the content to fluctuate between sessions and so this condition produces the highest performance in an immediate examination, when the test strongly overlaps with the same information that we were learning. So it works very well when what we have to learn is verbatim material, say a few lines in a play for tomorrow, but not so well when we have to use material a month after we learnt. In other words, if students need to remember information for only a short time—for example a few minutes or maybe a couple of hours— wider spacing's between learning sessions will not provide any gains over briefly spaced repetitions (as compared to situations that require long-term retention). Thus most school tests and examinations the way they are usually conducted, reward short and intermediate term recall rather than long term learning the very antithesis of the intent of education—the cramming effect not the learning.

Why do gaps between learning sessions increase retention? There could be at least three reasons.

1. Wider gaps between sessions entail extra mental and cognitive energy and such effort generates stronger memory traces and better recall.
2. Wider gaps create memory traces that are more varied than narrow gaps between sessions, producing manifold retrieval paths that aid recall.
3. Wider gaps between sessions produce more forgetting during the learning process, motivating us to use diverse and more effective coding strategies that aid recall.

The spacing effect is one of the ancient and best-accepted evidence in the field of learning and memory research. Amazingly, while it is one of the best accepted the spacing effect is also one of the least appreciated in the fields of by faculty and teachers.

One reason is that most students feel that cramming produces better results than spaced learning. Students who cram have an inflated sense of their skill to remember the repeated information.[16] Cramming give students a false sense that they know the material. Given this false sense, students often stop attending; they think they know the material, so they move on. Faculty and teachers are not any better. When a group of educationalists to were asked to

---

[16](Zechmeister and Shaughnessy (1980)

compare cramming and spaced learning they predicted that the cramming would produce 15% more learning than the spaced repetitions, when in reality the cramming produced 36% less learning than the spaced repetitions.[17] The upshot of this argument is that, although spaced learning is a highly effective learning method, both students and faculty have had a propensity to avoid its use.

What is the Right Spacing Interval?

Classic studies from the time of Ebbinghaus suggest that the best time to repeat is when you have almost forgotten the subject.

In general, most of the time we are looking for the long-term memory storage so long spacing is better.

---

[17](Rothkopf (1963)

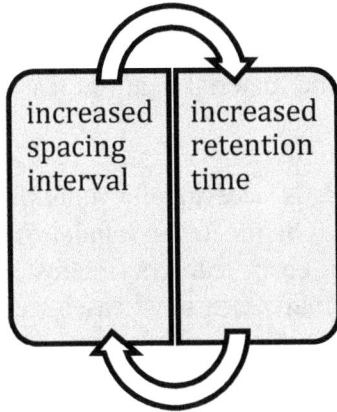

In the diagram, the arrows represent the relationship between spacing interval and retention time.

So what is the ideal spacing interval? A very recent large study shows that the optimal interval between study sessions should be 10-30% of the time before a test. If the retention interval (time until, say, a test) needed is one week, the spacing interval should be one to two days. If the retention interval is 100 days, the spacing interval, ideally, should be between 10-30 days.

But note how I used the word, "ideally". While the ideal spacing interval may maximize long-term remembering, we don't have to be tied to the ideal to get learning benefits. In fact, most of the time we are studying it is because we need to take exams or tests, not because we are trying to promote our long-term learning.

The optimal gap between study sessions is likely to be about 10-30% of the study-test delay. That is, your final exam is 10 weeks away so you need to study between one and three week intervals, but no less than a week's interval. So, if you want to remember material from the first week of class on the final exam (say ten weeks after you start the program), you should read it again a week or two after you studied it and then at the same intervals and finally close to the examination. If you want to know the optimal distribution of your study time, you need to decide how long you wish to remember something. If your goal is to remember something for life then it is not enough to study a subject once. You should study the material again at least a year after your first exposure.

Expanding spacing's is occasionally more difficult to achieve than consistent spacing. On the other hand, expanded study intervals may be useful to keep learners interested over long practice sequences. To summarize, in most cases we can use both types of spacing's, but expanding spacing's may have some benefit when we provide no feedback or relearning. We should remember that longer spacing intervals tend to be better than shorter ones if you want to remember for long time, not just to take a test. We can also space repetitions by just a day. There appears to be a great advantage even for one-day delays. If this is not feasible, we can use 4-hour spacing's instead of 2-hour spacing's, 1-hour spacing's instead of 15-minute spacing's and 10-minute spacing's instead of an immediate repetition. The key is to extend the time between relearning.

People learn and people forget. We as learners need to maximize learning, but also to minimize forgetting. We can learn things relatively rapidly, but true proficiency takes time and lots of learning effort as discussed in our previous rule on practice.

A Few Tips for Spacing Learning

1. Repetitions are effective in supporting learning. Spaced repetitions help minimize forgetting for the long term, while creating minor and temporary difficulties during learning. When we provide spaced repetitions on the job, the forgetting curve becomes a learning-and-forgetting curve. The additional learning can help maintain high levels of long term remembering.
2. Spacing repetitions are more effective than cramming for long-term retention. The closer in time learning is delivered to the situations when it is needed, the less forgetting will be a factor.

The less forgetting, the more you will be able to remember what you learned and apply it to your work.

3. Spacing between learning sessions is particularly useful if long-term retention is the goal. Adequate gaps between sessions can minimize forgetting. Long learning sessions can create weariness, distraction, and cognitive processing that is less deep and effective than the ideal. It's imperative to understand that the "spacing effect" denotes repetition of the learning. So, though it may be helpful to space unrelated learning sessions to avoid fatigue, the spacing effect goes beyond fatigue prevention.

4. Gradually expanding the length of spacing's can create benefits, but these benefits generally do not outperform consistent spacing intervals. Distributing learning sessions over time, whether these sessions repeat learning points or not induce extra studying. This is especially true if learners feel that the material will require prerequisite knowledge. Learners who have been away from material may be inspired to refresh their knowledge before they go on to the next topic. They know from experience that if they don't understand what came before, the new material just won't make any sense.

5. One way to utilize spacing is to change the definition of a learning event to include the connotation that learning takes place over time—real learning doesn't usually occur in one-time events.

6. The formula is to have agap of 10 to 30% of the retention interval i.e. time interval for retaining the knowledge such as time to a test.

The Art of Learning

In virtually every type of course or sport that we study, there are many topics and subtopics, be it a course on the nervous system, English Grammar, calculus or baseball. Most of us study by first focusing on one topic, and then when we complete that topic we go to the next. This type of learning in blocks appears very effective, but there is a far more effective alternative.

Let's say you are learning a particular set of math problems. The typical method would be to try out the same type of problem over and over until we become proficient. The process feels natural and is one that we are all accustomed to. But this intuition is a fallacy. In fact mixing up material we learn within and across subjects enhance learning.

This mixing up works very well for learning sports that is if you are learning tennis it will be best to mix up serving with learning backhand or forehand. In fact, you learn the most when you use all the different aspects of tennis, rather than just learning one thing at a time before moving to the next. The world's top tennis coaches agree that although there are many components required to develop the complete tennis player, it is not the individual pieces that make the player but the seamless integration of these parts.
Each of these pieces has their own methods, tips and traps but focusing on one element is not the usual strategy when you learn the game. In fact most lessons, both in the early stage and especially later on, interleave all the different elements including playing the whole game as the learning plan, a "holistic" approach.

A player does not play the game with only technique. Even on ostensibly purely technical issues, the other components are inextricably entangled. For example, take the common condition where a player is in the final set and sets up the point for a winner. Rather than putting the ball (even though they have practiced that skill a thousand times) they hit it out or into the net. Technically, one can explain why the shot went wrong. But usually the reason could be emotional. It could be physical fatigue. Thus in sports, mixing up learning elements of what one needs to be proficient in within the whole is a very natural part of training.

Even for training skills within the game, the approach is not to just practice serving a ball over and over for an entire session and then, come the next session, just practice volleying or backhand strokes. Learning skills are intermixed in a typical practice session. In one session the student learns to serve for a bit, then tries volleying and practices different strokes. The approach feels natural because the goal is not to be proficient in one thing but learn to play the whole game. No one wants to be perfect in just one element they know it has limited value.

A simple experiment with college basketball players demonstrates the power of this principle. College baseball players were set up to practice hitting three types of pitches (fastball, curveball, and change-up), and the 45 practice pitches were either divided in sets by type of pitch (15 fastballs, 15 curveballs, and 15 change-ups) or mixed up (fastball, curveball, change ups). When the players were tested as though they were playing in a real game, the group who received the mixed up pitch training performed better than those who received sequential training.[18]
This seems intuitive when playing sports but may seem alien when it comes to school subjects. But the same principle holds whether one is learning math, language or sports. The reason for the intuition gap is obvious: the purpose of learning is not so well defined as learning a sport.

Why study math, science and English or any other subject? Students, faculty, and teachers are not clear about why it is difficult to engage in "Holistic" learning. Systems of learning have become

---

[18](Hall, K. G., Domingues, D. A., & Cavazos, R. (1994). Contextual interference effects with skilled baseballplayers. Perceptual and Motor Skills, 78, 835–841.)

so focused on the parts that the sum of the parts is much smaller than the whole the opposite of what we would like it to be.

So if we want to learn, understanding why and what we want to learn helps set the goals. In turn it makes the need to not only learn different subjects but also to put them together and use them become self-evident and not counter-intuitive. This principle of mixing up and alternating different topics and problems is called "interleaving" and it works the same way as mixing up serving and volleying in tennis. It makes it clear that the whole learning experience is more than the sum of its parts.

Does mixing up how you learn improve performance in academic subjects?

- There are quite a few studies that have begun to explore this question.3-year-old children were shown new objects one at a time and told each object's name. Similar objects had the same name. Children who saw the objects in a sequence that was mixed up than when they were shown the objects of the a series were shown first and then objects from the second series and so on were better able to name hitherto unseen objects on an ensuing test.[19]

- Learning the style of 12 famous artists based on looking at six paintings by each artist. Mixing up the artists' paintings, rather than presenting them sequentially six by one artist and then six by the next etc., increased ability to identify the artist style later. The group that learnt by viewing paintings in a mixed sequence outdid those who studied one artist at a time by 59% to 36%. Nearly 80% of individuals performed better with learning by mixing the artists painting than learning in sequence.[20]

---

[19](Vlach, H. A., Sandhofer, C. M., & Kornell, N. (2008) The spacing effect in children's memory and category induction. Cognition, 109, 163–167).
[20](Kornell, N., & Bjork, R. A. (2008). Learning concepts and categories: Is

- Learning how to calculate the volumes of four different solids: One group of students received Tutorial followed by Practice solving volumes for a specific shape of solid, then they received another tutorial and practice trial problems for the next type of solid etc. (This is the typical sequential or one skill at a time learning.) The second group of students first studied all four tutorials and then finished all the practice problems, with the stipulation that every set of four consecutive problems included one problem for each of the four kinds of solids. In other words the problems were mixed up. One week after the second session, all the students took a test in which they answered two fresh problems for each of the four types of solids. During the learning period performance was better with sequential learning and practice than the mixed up learning practice, but this advantage radically reversed on the follow up test. Those taught by mixing it up (interleaving) had retention levels of 63 per cent when tested a week later compared with a 20 per cent retention rate in those taught in a block without mixing it up a 43 % improvement almost tripling the retention rate.

- In a very similar comparison the results were the same for young students taught to decipher four kinds of mathematics problems relating to prisms and a test 1 day later showed that students who learnt using a sequence of mixing up problems rather than learning problems in sequence did twice as well 77 % vs. 38 %.[21]

- In medicine mixing up worked when learning to read electrocardiograms in diagnosing heart conditions. Two groups of students studied how to interpret EKG's one group learnt with a set of mixed examples of EKG's and the

spacing the "enemy of induction" Psychological Science 19, 585-592)
[21](Taylor, K., & Rohrer, D. (2010). The effect of interleaving practice. Applied Cognitive Psychology, 24, 837–848).

other learnt how to read EKG's by studying examples of a particular problem and then another set etc. The accuracy was vastly better for the group that studied by mixing it up, 47% for mixing it up and 30% for sequential learning.[22]

In each instance, "mixing it up" led to a higher rate of learning.

It is not just mixing it up but also using larger sets of problems that can help students achieve a better result. An experiment in math by Rickard Lau and Paschler, students calculated 24 diverse multi-digit multiplication problems, each of which they repeated 15 times.

One group were given the problems in 8 sets of 3 (3 problems 15 times each before moving to the next set of 3), and the other group worked the problems in 2 blocks of 12. The group who had larger block sizes made more errors during the training period, but they outdid the smaller set size group on a test given after an interval. This suggests that training on small problem sizes allows people to learn more easily—it is easier to remember 3 things at a time than 12. In a way this is not dissimilar to why having a gap between learning sessions (spacing) works. Practicing material that is "fresh on your mind" in small chunks provides minimal benefits: the immediate accessibility of an answer means that further practice isn't engaging any actual conceptual/computational processes.[23]

This conclusion has been shown in many studies in math and many other academic fields. Just as we see in sports the learning curve is slower during practice, with more errors occurring during practice for the group that learnt by mixing it up; but performance on

---

[22](Hatala RM1, Brooks LR, Norman GR. Practice makes perfect: the critical role of mixed practice in the acquisition of ECG interpretation skills. Adv Health Sci Educ Theory Pract. 2003;8(1):17-26.)
[23](Rickard, T.C., Lau, J.S., & Pashler, H. (2008). Spacing and the transition from calculation to retrieval. Psychonomic Bulletin & Review, 15, 656-661.)

subsequent tests is much better for the group that learns by mixing it up than for the group that studied sequentially.

Sequential versus interleaved practice

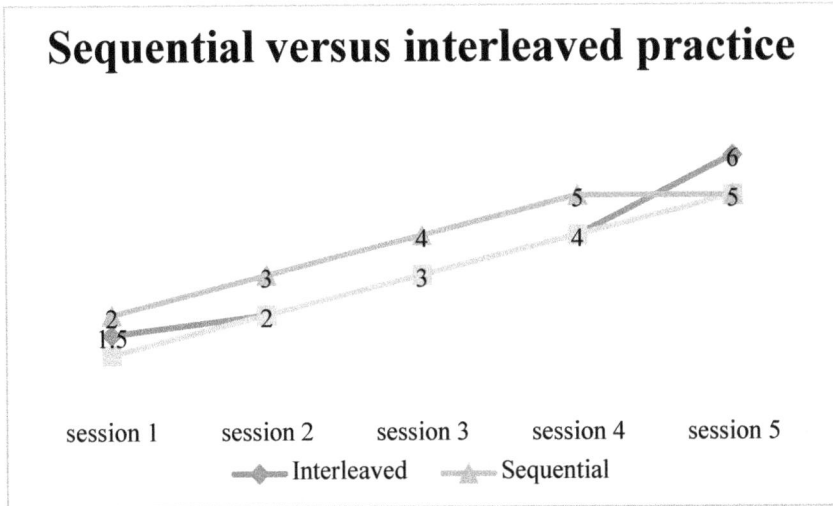

session 1   session 2   session 3   session 4   session 5
◆ Interleaved   ▲ Sequential

Figure shows that learning curve can be slower for interleaved learning than sequential

But the retention can be better.

This approach has the potential to reduce overall learning time. An early classroom study compared predictable mathematics instruction with an analogous instruction but in which some class-like lectures, was replaced with worked example training. The results showed a dramatic acceleration in learning such that students finished a 3-year course sequence in 2 years with as good or better final test performance.[24]

The most common explanation is that just like in the sports analogy mixing it up gives you a broader understanding and the skill to figure out which solution will work for a precise problem. If you are solving problems of the same kind in sequence once you know how to do it, but you do not when to and do not spend much effort

[24](Zhu, X., and Simon, H.A. (1987). Learning mathematics from examples and by doing. Cognition and Instruction, 4, 137-166.)

in recalling and contrasting information to find the right solution. This is just like a baseball player who knows how to hit one type of pitch but not another or a tennis player who is great at serving but poor in volleying.

Mixing it up means more effort to recall information from long-term memory and the switching allows comparisons between problems and leads to a better ability to connect different ideas and come up with solutions. This mixing or interleaving slows the learning curve by requiring more effort in switching between learning strategies, or motor skills in the case of sports, but this increased level of difficulty is desirable in that it increases learning by making you and your brain work more.

Even simple change in perceptual cues can increase difficulty, which is a good way to increase learning. The individual difficulty of processing perceptually dissimilar information leads people to participate in more concentrated processing strategies, which results in higher recall for that material. The approach has been confirmed in language learning, math, and many other subjects. Mixing it up leads to better long-term retention of content, and also leads to better ability to connect the learning to other things and transfer knowledge to other material; it may even enhance creativity.

Interleaving and Long Term Memory

Imagine a scenario in which you practice different examples of a single type of math problem for an hour in class. By the end of the hour, it may seem to you that you mastered this type of math problem. On a test the next week, much to your dismay, the benefit may not be evident. In fact the performance during your learning practice is not always representative of long-term learning if you do not know how to apply the right response or skill to the right situation.

The Art of Learning

In contrast to the story told above, if you mix up and interleave your practice your learning will be much stronger and deep at the end. Learning in sets and in sequence leads to short-term gains that are deceptively compelling; it feels right to learn this way, but it is wrong.

In the short-term, difficulties slow the learning curve, but prolong the forgetting curve in the long-term. Gaps between sessions, as in learning by spacing and interleaving, creates difficulties and slows learning pace but improves learning for the longer term.

But it is this difficulty that benefits you, the student, in the long-term; learning with some level of effort leads to less forgetting and more long-term retention. But therein lays the problem: everyone prefers the feeling of quick progress. The route to sustained development feels uncomfortable. We have to delay satisfaction. We might look bad. So we don't do it.

This means that instead of studying by first knowing what we need to learn and learning by mixing it up in a manner akin to sport, we instead work out and develop skills individually without much thought about the final outcome.

Mixing it up still needs a basic level of understanding and knowledge, of course. You cannot play tennis if you do not know how to properly hold a racket. In the same way interleaved learning works only when a there is a baseline level of skill. The amount of instruction and practice that you initially receive with each skill or task will affect the degree to which mixing it up will enhance performance. In fact, when you are learning a new concept or problem type (e.g., how to solve linear algebra problem) you would naturally begin with learning the basic concept and practice with that concept or problem type. You have to learn to hit with the bat before you practice against different pitches if you are a baseball player.

The question is how much initial practice is enough, and when should you start mixing things up. Given that skill level and task difficulty have been shown to moderate the benefits of mixing it up in learning a sport, it seems likely that they do the same for other types of learning. If so, the amount of initial instruction and skill practice should interact with the benefits of mixing it up such that more pre-training should be required if you are new to the area of study, as well as for more complex skill tasks.

A small study serves as a guide: This was a study of fifth and sixth graders learning fractions. During practice, students were taught diverse ways to characterize fractions, such as with pie charts, and line diagrams. Practice was either in sequence by sets (e.g., students worked with pie charts first, then line segments etc.), interleaved, or first by sequence and then interleaved. They were then tested before and after practice. Those who had poor background did best when they practiced in sequence alone and when they first studied in sets followed by mixing it up. This outcome suggests that interleaving may be most beneficial only after a certain level of competency has been achieved.

We do not know how well this works when subjects are totally different, or if the shifting happens under very short time conditions, but the basic principle is to mix things up when possible and, preferably, switch between subjects and between different types of problems within the same subject.

But here's the cool part: If you study, wait, and then study again by recall, the longer the wait, the more you'll have learned after this second study session. In addition if you now mix it up with something else you may make your learning even better. Bjork explains it this way: "When we access things from our memory, we do more than reveal it's there. It's not like a playback. What we retrieve becomes more retrievable in the future. Provided the retrieval succeeds the more difficult and involved the retrieval, the more beneficial it is."

A Few Tips for Mixing It Up

The Art of Learning

1. *Mix up practice.*
2. *When studying, don't focus on a single subject. Instead interleave a mix of subjects in a single session.*
3. *Mixing increases long term retention but slows learning. Don't get frustrated if you start slowly, the payoff will be worth it.*

The Art of Learning

Humans have always learned from each other and from their interaction with the world around them. Children can pick up behaviours just by watching videos or cartoons and conversely if they see punishment for that behaviour in what they observe it reduces their inclination to imitate that behaviour. Even as adults we learn all the time by our engagement with peers and other adults in the real world and today through our links to the cyber world. This brings us to our next rule for learning:

When I was in high school I used to study sometimes with friends. If there was something that I could not understand, it was easier to ask a friend—they could usually explain a concept or a problem in a more understandable form than a teacher could. A teacher was also not available, especially when we are learning at home or away from school. I also did not feel that I was being evaluated or judged when I asked a friend for help, whereas asking a teacher could feel intimidating.

It also helped me reinforce my learning when I tried to teach one of my peers. Trying to explain a problem helped me see it with greater clarity and even lead to changing misconceptions about the problem. Occasionally none of us knew how to address the question or problem and in these instances dialogue and debate amongst us helped.

Yes, we competed but we also helped each other out. We all had our strengths and weaknesses but we worked together and helped each other out as we prepared for examinations. Examinations, especially state or National exams, were key to moving ahead in life when I was growing up in India. Each exam was the gatekeeper between the next step and us in our academic progression. My group of friends and I would often get together and work on math or science problems, comparing and sharing notes as way to help each other learn.

The Art of Learning

Today, as I watch my children and their friends, I see the same pattern except they do not meet, they chat using any number of tools, Facebook, Google hangout and What's App. This form of collaborative learning has moved from face-to-face to the online world. The power of peer and collaborative learning is as powerful today as it ever was maybe even more so.

And it is not just humans that learn from and influence each other. This collaborative learning is seen amongst fish, birds, and mammals. A very interesting study illustrates this type of learning: Monkeys living in small groups in the wild were allowed to select food coloured either pink or blue. One colour for each group was contaminated with aloe to provide it an innocuous but unpleasant flavour.

After a few mealtimes, the aloe was removed from the food, but the monkeys learnt to avoid the colour that had previously been contaminated with aloe. They wouldn't go near it. But that behaviour transformed when monkeys from one group, say those who ate pink food, tried to fit in with another group of monkeys who ate the blue food. The monkeys that had been eating the pink food soon switched to eating blue food. This shows the social influence on learning is similar to what we see in humans and it is an innate trend even in animals. Learning from peers is not uniquely human and is indeed a very powerful mode of learning.

Not just monkeys but whales also learn the same way. Humpback whales forage by blowing bubbles below schools of fish, which makes them cluster together to avoid swimming through the bubbles. Then the whales can swallow a very large helping of fish in one go. In 1980, a whale in the Gulf of Maine (off New England) was seen smacking its tail on the surface of the ocean before feeding on sand lance fish. After three or four times of slapping its tail it would dive for the fish. This appeared to make it easier for the whale to get more fish. In that first year (1980) the behaviour was seen just once, but by 2007 more than 37% of the whales were doing the same behaviour. This behaviour had spread geographically and had passed down over numerous generations. The behaviour was learnt from other whales through *peer learning*.

Peer learning, in which colleagues and friends explain concepts to one another, demands clarification, elaboration, and reconceptualization of material, all of which promotes learning for everyone involved. Humans have always learned from each other. But for a long time—until the advent of the Web, Google, ITunes, YouTube and pervasive access to digital media—schools have had a real and almost complete monopoly on the business of education and learning. Our learning, both as children and as adults, is enhanced by either a professional or an experienced peer, someone who knows the space, the territory and language. But teachers and specialists are not essential to our ability to learn. Specialists are great but not always available and or needed. We should learn as much from specialists as we can when we have the opportunity but not just look or wait for them.

But through the advent of the open access to vast educational assets and free or inexpensive communication tools, clusters of people can learn together outside as well as inside traditional educational institutions. These open educational resources, MOOCs and free communication platforms such as Skype, Google Hangouts enable clusters of people to learn together outside as well as inside formal academic institutions.

Children can learn by themselves with their friends

A dozen years ago a computer scientist, Mitra, in Delhi carried out a fascinating study. He took a personal computer and placed it in a room full of children who had never seen or operated a computer. He then watched them from the outside. What he observed was a compelling story of children playing and figuring out how to use the computer even though they were not provided with any instructions. The children were learning by doing, helping each other and experimenting, a form of desirable self-learning. They learnt by discovery and by playing. In a short time they were learning to paint, play games and create documents.

In a subsequent study the same group of scientists placed computers in a kiosk at a playground in a village. In April 2002, five Minimally Invasive Kiosks (MIE) kiosks were opened in villages of the Sindhudurg district of Maharashtra State, India. In a span of a few months, many of the students who played on the computers were able to pass tests on computer science exams even without teacher input. This led the authors to try out an experiment. One group (Experimental group) played on computers at the kiosk. A second group had no exposure to computers and a third group went through a formal curriculum on computers. 87% of the Experimental Group passed the practical examination. The highest overall score in the Experimental Group was 62%, almost the same as the Group that received formal computer instruction (69%) and significantly better than in the control group (14%) that did not receive any instruction or chance to play at the kiosk.

In a follow-up, they asked whether children could learn math from using the computer so they loaded it with math-learning games. The games covered numbers, shapes, sizes, quantities, addition, subtraction, division, multiplication, and algebra. The children were allowed to play the games on the computer without adult supervision. Children played, discovered and learnt on their own. The children did better on tests and their performance was related to the time spent on the kiosk. Obviously this did not work for everyone but the study shows that children playing with their friends can productively use a learning environment.

But how much can children learn without teachers who are experts in the subject?

In unsupervised situations such as the Hole-in-the-Wall observation, children do what they like doing and therefore are inclined to shine in their specific areas of interest. Not everybody

156

learns the same thing or to the same extent. Some individuals may benefit, others may not; and the gap could reflect desire and motivation.

Another experiment with 10–14 year old Tamil-speaking children showed they could learn limited amount of basic molecular biology by themselves using a public computer facility. But an untrained teacher could still help by proving supervision and encouragement to the children. The students did better with this little bit of supervision showing even more improvement with a helper even though he or she was not knowledgeable about the subject. The learning outcomes were similar to children at a nearby state government school who were taught molecular biology by a teacher. In fact these children performed almost equal to their peers at a private urban school.

Could this learning be used as a tool in regular schools?

I had the privilege of watching a class that promotes self-directed collaborative learning at Macpherson Secondary School (Singapore) with Chew Lee Teo. They use a knowledge-building approach in which students and teachers collaborate, brainstorm and learn together. They used a simple experiment to enhance learning and serve as a focal point. The learning was very interactive, with questions and answers building a knowledge base for the entire class. The teacher served as a mediator and facilitator rather than the one with all the answers. The learning environment became one that the children were engaged in and more important connecting to their own real world experience. In other words, the learning became less based on a compulsion to learn and more on a desire to learn. They worked on laptops with access to the Internet and software that promoted learning. The software and the teacher became the tools to excite, adapt and improvise learning and build context to the learning exercise. The entire class became a self-learning environment.

The Art of Learning

Self-Learning

Learning can be of three kinds, learning that we desire, learning that we need, and learning that we have to do (compulsory learning). The latter is often what children feel that they learn at school and the former what they do on their own time. Unfortunately, compulsory learning is required. So maybe we need to work on making learning desirable and interesting.

Self-learning happens best when there is a desire to learn. We have evolved by organizing ourselves into structures that adapt, learn and evolve. In other words, we have evolved through self-organizing. Every time we meet people, we are learning about each other or the world around us. This environment for organizing ourselves to learn has been called the self-organizing learning environment (SOLE). SOLEs are everywhere. A conversation between strangers is self-organizing *and learning*, as we learn about something or each other. The spaces around people interacting and conversing are also an environment, though not explicitly a learning one.

While we are always self-organizing to learn or accomplish things, one place that SOLEs do not always exist is in learning institutions. Building an environment and structure to develop self-learning is what schools and colleges should strive for. The Macpherson school experiment is one that shows the development of a self-organizing teacher facilitated learning environment. The learning environment and the class was a study in excitement and energy.

The more schools and universities move learning from a compulsory learning characteristic to a desirable learning stage we will get closer to learning for the soul. Many of these efforts, which leverage technology and the desire to learn, have the potential to disrupt traditional learning structures and models; but it is more than likely they will supplement, transform, transplant and enhance learning for all.

The Art of Learning

A wealth of resources are now available that promote and help you to build this form of collaborative self-learning. Here is a sample:

Rheingold U
One particularly intriguing model (and a very useful start) is Rheingold U. This is an entirely online learning community, providing short courses of about five weeks, mixing live sessions and asynchronous dialogues through forums, blogs, wikis and other social media. The founder of Rheingold taught at University of California Berkley and at Stanford. The subject matter and the methods taught here could be a starting point for learning how to use modern media and the wide world of information to enhance learning.

Peeragogy
Peeragogy is another resource for people who want to learn with each other. They provide the "How to" structure for people to build their own peer-learning program. The web site is a wonderful resource of useful information on how to build and construct learning networks. It is a model of peer-to-peer (P to P) learning that helps develop and support build self-directed learning.

Also, the Peeragogy handbook is a practical guide to co-learning that invites discussion and is managed by a community of editors.

P2P U:
This is a community of learners whose slogan speaks for itself: "learning by everyone, for everyone, about almost anything, completely free."
It is a university for the web. It offers massive open online courses (MOOCS). At this point in time there are only a few subjects on offer, but the idea is clear and the resources are available to build communities of learning. It shows you how to build your own courses and see if it works.

159

How do you build a peer learning community for young adults?

Step 1: Know your goal.

What is it you want to learn? Is it mathematics or biology or computer science or hacking or a language?

Step 2: Build your own learning plan and pathway to reach this goal.

This helps you identify your special and unique learning style, studying interest and capacity. You need this to develop your personal plan. The question you need to ask yourself:

What is my learning style and what methods help me learn and what type of help will I need?

Step 3: Are there networks in one form that are available or will you have to develop one to fit your need?

If there are networks that fit your needs it will be easiest to join them rather than create new networks. An example is the Peer Learning Association at University of Wisconsin. The group is a student organization that launches and runs free small group study meetings led by Peer Facilitators. Here students assess their understanding of course material by discussing key topics to fellow classmates in an informal venue.

Penn State also offers a variation called Guided Study Groups (GSG) for a select number of courses. The courses are enabled by other students to study with their peers in a learning environment. The student facilitators are undergraduate students who have previously taken and met success in the course.

Step 4: Create a new learning network or group.

The Art of Learning

First, check out the websites for Peeragogy and P2P U to learn the necessary steps to form your own peer-learning group. If you are in college or high school and on a physical campus it may be best to see if you can form a study group there. If you can, this will be helped further if you can find a senior student who has done well in the course you are interested in to guide you. If you present yourself and your goal in a thoughtful and attractive way, this will help you to build effective connections with friends and colleagues and to create a learning group.

If you are not part of a school or college then creating networks can be based on finding other interested people to join. Networks can span across different subjects, across a city, or across national and global boundaries. There is an abundance of tools now available to build collaborative networks. It is enticing to seize a group of elaborate tools and bring the group into a complex tool setting. The problem is not about finding the tools but finding the people who can work and learn together.

When it comes to using collaborative tools, the rule of thumb is to use ones that are easy, commonplace and need the least amount of learning to get started. When the group gets more comfortable, new tools can then be introduced and, if they are effective, then they too become part of the natural scheme of things. The introduction of tools should be the facilitator of the goals and learning objectives, not the aim.

Tools

Synchronous	Google+ Hangouts Skype Google Docs forums

Asynchronous	Blackboard Collaborate Google Docs Adobe Connect Wkis Forums

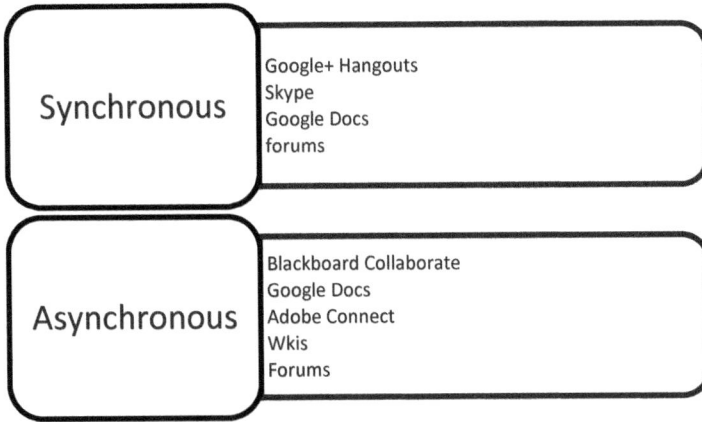

How to Build a SOLE

1. Search for what to study.

2. Collect material and seek out expert opinions and useful information.

3. Create a repository to study.

4. Explore and study individually.

5. Come together as group to discuss the material. This could be synchronous or even asynchronous.

The Art of Learning

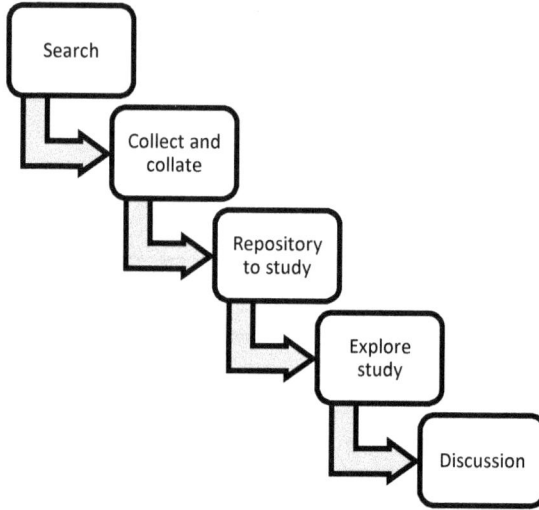

These self-learning steps can even be followed with groups of young students.

The Art of Learning

When I was in medical school more than 30 years ago, the best students (and those predicted to be successful) would be those individuals who accumulated the most amount of factual knowledge that they could then apply in taking care of patients. This was equally true in most other fields of study. Turn to today, now we are swamped by an ever-accumulating tsunami of information that is easily accessible but difficult to put in perspective. Information is at our fingertips but how to apply remains distant. This has reduced the value of rote memorization of facts and increased the value of the ability to conceptualize, search, analyse, synthesize and apply knowledge. Learning today and for the future has to move beyond memorization of facts to conceptual understanding and application in collaborative settings.

We begin with a fundamental aspect of learning and retention: understanding.

Learning with Understanding

The National Research Council in the US has noted seven principles of learning, which are very applicable to today's knowledge-based world including the world of medicine.[25]

1. Learning with understanding is facilitated when knowledge is related to and structured around major concepts and principles of a discipline.
2. A learner's prior knowledge is the starting point for effective learning.
3. Metacognitive learning (self-monitoring) is important for acquiring proficiency.
4. Recognizing differences among learners is important for effective teaching and learning.

---

[25](Learning and Understanding: Improving Advanced Study of Mathematics and Science in U.S. High Schools (2002) National Academies Press.)

5. Learners' beliefs about their ability to learn affect learning success.
6. Practices and activities in which people engage during learning shape what is learned.
7. Socially supported interactions strengthen one's ability to learn with understanding.

Meaningful learning opens up more questions, more attempts at answering, more unknowns, and more questions that lead to creative thinking. Many trials have shown that students who are randomly assigned to conditions that encourage deep explanations do much better than when they are assigned to comparison circumstances that give the students same content, but without the need to build explanations. This works for students of all ages in these from fourth grade to college and subjects that range from science, history, mathematics, and statistics. The benefits are seen whether the assessment is just basic or factual and even more when it tests deep and fundamental knowledge. Comprehension and learning improve from training to ask deep-level questions while reading text, listening, or studying material. Once you learn that asking questions is okay, curiosity returns and questions flow.

Besides teaching how to ask questions, teaching students to think aloud, explain their thoughts, and link the material to previous knowledge and experiences produce better understanding, deeper explanations and less repetition of material. This works when you, the learner, are studying by yourself and maybe even better when you have to explain to your friends. **So ask yourself questions, work with friends or parents to seek answers, use the whole World Wide Web; be curious.**

The excellence of self-explanations increases when students see others provide high-quality explanations. These patterns give students guidance on how to develop better self-explanations. In many subjects there may well be multiple valid justifications, permitting students to evaluate diverse points of view and trails of reasoning. To put it simply, watching others ask questions and going to debates that elicit explanations, is a good way to learn.

Learning a concept in a concrete form makes it difficult for students to use that knowledge in a different context (e.g., to solve a problem in a related field). But, when students are introduced to a concept using an abstract depiction, they struggle slightly more to master the concept initially, but are then able to use their new knowledge effectively in an altered context. It seems that the greater early trouble in grasping abstract instruction is rewarded by a greater ability to apply the concept to very diverse situations.

The acquisition and retention of knowledge has many domains or levels of depth.

The first and the simplest are remembering and in essence refer to retaining facts. Unfortunately retaining facts without understanding is difficult and has a very limited life span. The next level is comprehension or understanding. This level is shown by the ability to re-convey in one's own words the meaning of the information.

Understanding serves as the prelude to being able to analyse, compartmentalize or break down the knowledge; to be able to judge, evaluate, or value the knowledge and then be able apply the knowledge to a new context; or to synthesize by integrating with other information. When learning medicine or other similar domains of work, this ability to use the knowledge is critical— without it facts by themselves have limited value.

In addition, the ability to then use this knowledge to create new knowledge becomes invaluable and is a key element in the training to becoming a scientist. One element that is essential in this progression of knowledge acquisition is *reasoning*. Reasoning is to infer. To infer is to draw conclusions from data, information or premises. The term *logic* is generally used to describe the principles of good reasoning. It used to be a subject that was taught in schools but one that is now rarely formally taught but one is expected to intuit. Logic when it is informal is seen or described as critical thinking. Logic does not evaluate how people use reasoning or why they reason in a particular manner but it tells us how to reason.

One of the main principles in logic is whether the conclusions follow from the assumptions. Formal logic is the systematic application of principles of logic. Formal systems of logic are specially assembled systems for carrying out proofs. The principles of logic are universal and apply to all fields whether it is medicine, biology, or economics. There are many strands of logic but a fair amount of formal logic dates back conceptually to Aristotle. Deductive logic refers to conclusions where when all the premises are true there can be no other way that the conclusion can be false. The fundamental element in deductive reasoning is syllogism where one suggestion is inferred from two premises each of which has one term in common with the conclusion.

For example:
All plants are alive.
The rose is a plant.
The rose is alive.

If the premise is true, the conclusion is true; and if the premise is false, the conclusion is false. In medicine and in many other forms of science, deductive logic is difficult. But another type of logic, inductive logic, is more applicable. Deductive logic is absolutist. It offers black and white standards in which the conclusion either follows from the premises or it does not. Inductive logic or reasoning is not absolutist or certain but provides a quantitative range of possibilities. Deductive reasoning is seen as more top-down from a general principle to the specific whereas inductive reasoning is bottom up. Thus is medicine one makes an observation to hypotheses generation to a probabilistic conclusion.

Elaboration

The Art of Learning

We are by nature curious but we tend to lose our sense of inquisitiveness over time. How often do you catch yourself thinking, "just give me the answer," or, "tell me what I should know for the exam"? It seems that we have become too impatient to think.

Now how often do you ask questions like: "Tell me why? "Or, "Why not?" Who do you think asks these latter types of questions? Not college students. Not high school students. No, just little kids. Little kids are curious. They learn about the world by questioning. "Mommy what is that? Why he is doing that? How much longer? And how do we respond. "Not now," "I don't know, ask your mom," and "later." We neither answer their questions, nor do we ask them a question. We end up discouraging their curiosity and maybe in many ways reduce their learning. Instead we try to teach them words to memorize, alphabets to learn, and numbers to count. No doubt important but just not enough by itself. Sustaining their innate curiosity maybe more worthwhile.

Let's think about why questions are important. For one thing, when no questions are asked no answers are found. Imagine a world in which no questions are asked. What would we know? Without questions there is no thinking, no search for the answer. Thinking is driven by questions not answers. The people who develop a field always start with the questions, challenge the dogma and seek answers. Without questions any field of study would never have developed in the first place. In fact, every human endeavour into new fields always starts with curiosity-driven questions for which answers are either not available or are unsatisfactory. In any field that is vibrant and alive, every answer leads to more questions. When there are no more interesting questions, what happens? The intellectual energy, interest, and growth dry up. Questions are the foundation that builds reason. Questions stimulate thought. Questions help conceptualize the material.
When a question is properly defined can generate analysis, synthesis and in fact promote creativity. Those sorts of questions commonly stem from: *why, what caused A, how did B happen,*

The Art of Learning

what if, what-if-not, why not, how does A compare to B, what is the evidence for C, and why is D important? Questions that stimulate deep explanations are best. For example, students can ask, "Why are bees needed?" or, "What will happen if there are no more bees?" The answers make you consider underlying biological principles. This is better than asking questions that test factual knowledge.

The process of asking and answering the right questions ought to be modelled by knowledgeable peers, but these days you can see it in a number of web sites. People now turn to Google, answers.com, Wikipedia and others to simply find answers for questions. The popularity of these sites seems to imply less need to think. But a little bit of reflection shows that they raise more questions and begin to show the limits of what we know.

Our approach at our school in Singapore requires students to raise questions when they discuss with each other, to clarify, engage and disagree. The students who have questions are thinking and learning. Asking questions is an objective marker of motivation and learning. The type and character of the questions that students ask reflect the depth of thinking they are doing. This allows more interaction reflection and stimulation of discussion. When I taught students in psychiatry at Duke, I used to like asking questions more as a way to engage and help them understand what we did not know. In retrospect I wonder if it would have been better to ask them to generate questions that could in turn stimulate more questions. Food for thought: I think questions are indeed a better way to engage and understand a topic.

Teaching yourself and prompting your children to ask questions and encouraging them to do so is critical to working in the new knowledge economy and in building the next generation of thought leaders. We need to teach our children and ourselves how to ask questions: Questions that can lead to more questions. There are many kinds of questions:

Questions to clarify: Tell me how does this work? Can you show me examples? What is the basis of this information? What are the assumptions? Does this work in all conditions? Where did you find this? Under this assumption will this work?

Questions that synthesize: How does this fit with what we previously learnt?

Questions that evaluate: Does this information change what we are planning? How does this relate to x? Does this affect y?

Questions that can lead to creativity: Can we use this elsewhere? What happens when we combine with this? Could it make a better widget?

There are as many ways to ask a question as there are ways to think. Our questions drive our thirst for knowledge. This is true for all kinds of learning. If we harness this sense of curiosity by learning to question we could improve learning.

One approach that has been used to harness this sense is called *elaborative questioning*. The key in this method is to build an explanation for an explicit fact, in other words to ask a "Why" question and answer it. The assumption is that this questioning increases learning by connecting to existing knowledge and promoting active linkage.

The Art of Learning

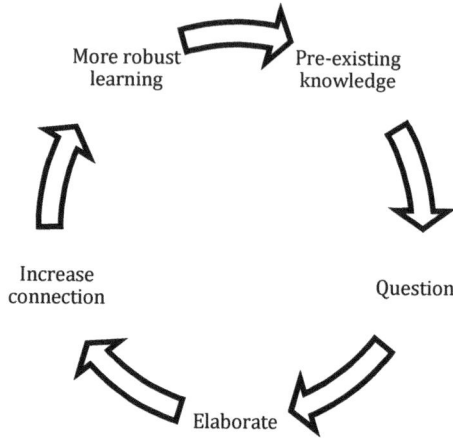

It may also promote assessment of the new information in terms of how similar or different it is to pre-existing knowledge. Interestingly, the studies in this area show that the larger and deeper the elaboration the greater the learning; the more it is self generated, the greater the learning; and it is also greater if there i greater wealth of pre-existing knowledge.

The method of elaborative interrogation may be an unwieldy term that makes you think of unpleasant encounters, but it is very effective for a very broad age range of individuals. It has been tried with elementary school, middle school, high school students and undergraduate students in a wide range of settings. It evens works for learning disabled children and high achieving children.

The extent of learning is indeed related to how much knowledge you already have on that subject.

For example, Canadian students presented with facts about Canadian provinces learnt the material much better than German students; and the converse was true for German students when it came to learning about German states as compared to Canadians. Elaborative interrogation had double the effect in their own knowledge domain than it did in the domain that they had limited knowledge. The most parsimonious reason is that the more pre-existing knowledge the greater the chance they can ask the right question and generate plausible answers.

The system works quite well for learning facts ranging from animals, human digestion to the solar system and beyond. In general it is an effective aid to learning facts and figures. The method helps retention for quite long periods of time all the way to 6 months. The nice thing about this approach is that it is very easy to learn; all you have to do is to ask why. Be like a child and learn to question.

Whether the approach will work when you are trying to learn more than facts depends on how good you are in asking the right questions and maybe on how much you already know about the subject.

Self-Explanation

This is a similar approach to elaboration here: connectivity to pre-existing knowledge is increased by consciously explaining how one went about solving problems. In this case, the question is, "How did you solve the problem?" Self-explanation could be for very specific prompts—*why did you do this?* —Or could be more general—*explain what this means to you.*

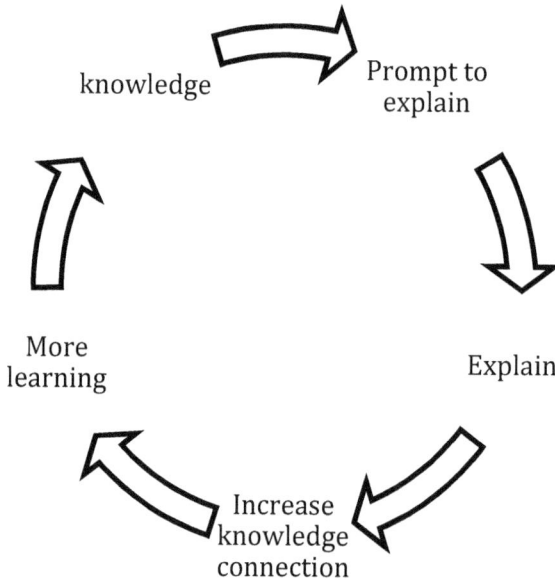

Self-explanation is most beneficial to the learning process if you do it at the same time as you are working on a problem—by talking to yourself. The approach is useful across a wide age range and has been tried in kindergartners and in college undergraduates.

The Art of Learning

Unlike the elaboration technique described earlier, this is more useful when it comes to problem solving. It is something to try when you are trying to work on algebra, math, or calculus problems. It is even useful for playing chess and other strategy games. It is designed to improve memory but also increase comprehension and increase connectivity to prior information. Unfortunately we do not have enough information about how long the benefits last. The presumption is that it does but the evidence is insufficient with regard to long-term benefit. This approach also needs minimal instruction; the approach is explained how you went about solving a problem. The better you can explain what you did, the more you learn and probably remember. It also allows transfer of knowledge from one situation to other comparable situations.

The Art of Learning

A very popular tool that is used to facilitate the learning process is a *concept map,* a map that links ideas together. This is because our brains are built to learn concepts even more than for memorizing knowledge.

From the time we are very young, even as babies, we begin to observe regular patterns within the world we see and hear. When language develops we build labels to describe what we observe. When we acquire the language of numbers we begin to assign symbols to describe the magnitude of the changes that we perceive. This early learning of patterns and objects and their nature is a discovery learning process. This is a time of great rapid and immersive learning by the child as it makes sense of its world.

After the child learns to associate sounds of word and visual symbols to objects and events, this new skill becomes the basis to expand knowledge beyond that which is directly observed. The new form of learning is mediated by language, and takes place by a process where new knowledge is obtained by exploring the world through questions and answers that link what they have discovered in the world of direct observation to the world beyond what they directly perceive.

This translation and extension of their knowledge of the world happens in the early stages by linking concrete objects and events to the new knowledge by using toys and other substitutes. Thus the child moves from the discovery learning process, where the attributes of concepts are developed directly by the child to the linguistic learning process, where concepts are developed using language.

Concepts and their links are the building blocks for knowledge in any field. In the English language there are over half a million words that can be used to describe concepts and their links. Words

175

in language are like atoms to molecules. You can build an almost infinite set of concepts and links that make up knowledge in any domain. It allows an infinite variety of creative development, and if we need to we can create new words to extend our creativity even more.

Individual children even at an early age begin to develop interests and preferences that, combined with their environment, lead to differentiation in their knowledge and motivation. This variation can lead to a continuum in how they learn. When children are motivated and have a sufficient base knowledge they are able to learn with an understanding that is meaningful learning; and when both motivations (interest and base knowledge) are diminished, it leads to increased attempts to memorize or learn by rote.

For meaningful learning to happen there should be three conditions: one, the person should have the capacity to use language to learn, which is the essential aspect to learning; second, the new knowledge has to be linked and built upon existing knowledge; and third, the person has to have an interest in understanding the new knowledge.

If you or the child has limited interest then it is more difficult to learn with meaning and understanding; but there are a few ways to help:

One technique is to build a relational system that ties what you or they know to what needs to be learnt. Concept maps are useful for this because they illustrate how one idea relates to another on a single page. First, we need to know the basic level of literacy and numeracy skills that the individual has, then the new concept that has to be taught must link to and use the skills that the person has as a way to sequence the learning tasks. Thus more knowledge can be built by developing conceptual frameworks in a particular domain.

The Art of Learning

If it is not and the person is going to be tested on this new knowledge, they have to resort to memorization. In other words they have to resort to rote learning. An indirect influence on both increasing learning with understanding and meaning and fostering interest and curiosity is how testing strategies and also instructional methods are used.

Testing and examination strategies have an enormous influence on how learning occurs and whether the learning will stick. Most tests ask for simple knowledge and facts that encourages memorization and rote learning. In early years some of it might be of use, but even that assumption is not without its detractors. Questions that require verbatim or very particular answers impedes learning with understanding in that the newly memorized information is simply compartmentalized rather than incorporated into existing knowledge.

The art and science of building questions is not easy and requires much effort but can be very valuable in helping meaningful learning. With testing we shape what we get; and tests of facts are easier to create then tests to build knowledge. This results in more tests with facts, requiring more memorization and less learning. Concept maps and linked testing can be a guide to build instructional strategies to promote effective meaningful learning.

Sum it up

The ability to summarize comes with understanding, it reflects the ability to separate the wheat from the chaff, discard irrelevant material and focus on the essentials. A good summation is greeted with cheers, but a poor one is infinitely more common. In school, teachers tell students to summarize what they learnt and that they need to summarize extend too many aspects of our life.

Summation or *summarization* is a device to aid understanding and remembering vast quantities of information that students have to learn. It involves finding the pearls of knowledge and distilling them into easily digestible and memorable content. Well-developed summaries provide the gist of the material, by excluding irrelevant content, focusing on the main points with clarity, resolving ambiguity and makes learning easier. A poorly developed summary is long rambling and imprecise.

Does summarizing work as a learning tool?

Summarizing and note taking has been proven to improve the performance of students more than verbatim copying. Students who simply copy verbatim have to discern the most important information in the text, but they do not have to understand, and write a summary in their own words. Those who summarize the information in their own words demonstrate a much stronger understanding of the material. Thus, putting pen to paper in the active process of summarizing and note taking produces a benefit over and above that of identifying important information.

Learning to summarize properly is skill that is worth developing

The ability to summate depends on the reading skill, writing ability and prior knowledge about the subject, so novices who are just beginning to learn a subject and young children have difficulty finding the main points and to copy from the text.

Watching others and practicing with feedback can help you learn summarization. There is a key caveat to keep in mind, however: summarizing seems simple but it is not. All too often, when students first start summarizing they usually write too much or copy verbatim, or if they are not sure they mix the main idea with the less important ones. These pitfalls can be avoided with a few mindful tips.

Some simple steps in learning how to summarize
1. Read slowly
2. Note the points that you think are important
3. Find the main idea
4. Find the ideas that support the main idea
5. Remove the ideas that are not important or not related to the main idea
5a. Erase repeat ideas or sentences
6. Start with the main idea and then pull together the supporting ideas and evidence

This is usually best done with feedback. Parents can teach their children by first asking them to say what the main idea is and then by questioning elicit the supporting ideas. Once the method is learnt it can be a useful technique.

Highlighting 'Highlighting'

Highlighting: Many have complained of it; others have embraced it with gusto. But few know how to use it. Highlighting, underlining, and marking are just tools; simple to use when you know how and useless when you do not. And just like anything valuable, use it too much and it is of no use.

When I was growing up in India, books were worshipped, and highlighting passages was unheard of and unseen. It would have been viewed as defacing books. But when I came to the US it was quite common to see words and sometimes entire passages in books that were highlighted or underlined. When you look at a book the highlighted sections stick out, and the eye focuses on the highlighted section, but does reading a highlighted piece help us learn?

Highlighting is widely used by students and teachers tell students to use highlighting as a tool to study. The technique is simple, easy to use and highlighting seems to make reading active and create the impression that the reader understood the material enough to mark it. But if there is so much variability in what students highlight or underline, it begs the question does highlighting work. Fortunately we have an answer.

Fowler and Barker[26] actually studied whether highlighting improves learning. They assigned students a paper that explored of all things boredom and city life. One group was told to read, the second to read and highlight as much as they desire, and the third were given a paper in which the elements that were important was already underlined (from the second group). They were all given the same amount of time to spend on their task. A week later they were allowed to review the material for ten minutes and then take a test on the material. There was no difference between the group that highlighted text and those who did not.

But if the highlighted material was part of the test, the person who highlighted that section did better. But if the test was on material that was not marked they did not do so well. The subjects who did the highlighting did better than those who just passively read the highlighted text. All the studies that have examined highlighting have shown the same pattern. If you highlight the relevant material you do well and too much highlighting or highlighting irrelevant material reduces performance.

[26] Fowler, Robert L.; Barker, Anne S.
Effectiveness of highlighting for retention of text material.
Journal of Applied Psychology, Vol 59(3), Jun 1974, 358-364

Highlighting draws focus to the material but if it is not the right material it has little value. The students who marked the most did poorly compared to those who highlighted selectively. Marking extensively needs little thought focus or energy but selective marking requires focus and understanding.

Highlighting by itself is of limited benefit unless the highlighting is a memory tool to bring understood material to the forefront. A small study amongst airmen provides evidence that this is the case. Airmen read a passage that was marked or unmarked. The marked material was useful and improved the performance of individuals who were more familiar with the material than those who were not.

Highlighting can also interfere with integrative understanding. A study compared three groups: one read the material, one read and underlined and then reviewed unmarked text at a later point, and the third marked and reviewed the marked text. The test contained both factual questions and inferential questions the three groups were similar in performance on the factual part of the test; but the group that did not mark or highlight did better than the other two groups on the questions that were inferential.

So maybe teaching students *how* to highlight may be what is needed. One tool that is used to make highlighting better is to limit the marking to no more than one line per paragraph. Studies show that students can be taught to highlight first by understanding and highlighting parsimoniously. This can make highlighting useful for reviewing material that is already digested and understood.

A Few Tips for Effective Highlighting:

1. Read first to understand.
2. Less is more. Be selective.
3. Highlight or mark just the material that helps bring back to memory, key material.

The Art of Learning

When we talk of learning, we usually end up talking about formal learning, conducted in classrooms. But learning happens all the time and in everything we do. In other words, most learning happens outside formal environments. Curiosity-based exploration drives experience-dependent learning. One of the best and most simple ways to learn is by remaining curious, discovering, experiencing, and exploring the world.

Humans are the most cognitively complex, adaptable and flexible of all animals. We are indeed born to learn and adapt. We learn and adapt to the specific physical and social environment into which we are born. We learn from our surroundings, the people that we interact with, and then with the tools that we acquire. We interact with the world and these interactions in turn shape our understanding of the world. We learn by seeing, hearing or perceiving the outside world and by language mediated learning process. We then make sense of the new information by placing it in the context of what we know. Thus we are constantly modifying our existing knowledge base. This in turn influences our behaviour. Our behaviour by its very nature generates new information that modifies our existing knowledge. This cycle of learning shapes who we are.

Learning in the real world is the result of continuous interaction between our surroundings and us. Learning is therefore not just acquiring simple information about a topic. It involves building, sharing, developing our thinking, behaviour and future perception. It also includes what we do, how we feel and what we see or hear. For example, interactions with diverse cultures and other people help us to learn awareness of feelings, both ours as well as those of others.

The net desired outcome of learning, whether it comes from the formal or informal means, is our ability to flourish in the

183

environment—in the working world or in social life. Learning and memory of that knowledge is essential for us to interact with the world around us, from recognizing friends, locations or performing actions. How we interact with the world is shaped by our experiences and our experiences are part and parcel of learning. Even though we talk as if perception learning and memory are distinct they are linked.

It is through experience that we learn from how our society works. If we see and experience ethical and transparent behaviour, we tend to emulate it. If we don't, we are more likely to follow unethical behaviour rampant in our midst. Thus the context and environment shape our knowledge and behaviour. We can gain a lot by experiencing multiple and diverse settings and environments beyond our own culture. Such experiences can broaden our outlook and enhance personal growth and tolerance.

There are different ways we can get our children to benefit more from experiential learning. A parent can exert more influence by telling his children to "do what I do" than to tell them, "do what I say, and not what I do." After all, the cultural mores and morality that are keys to early development come from watching what others do rather than just listening to exhortations.

We should make it a priority in early education to increase the likelihood of our children experiencing cultures other than ours. They will benefit by talking and interacting with people from other cultures and social backgrounds, where possible through travels. We should encourage our children to be like Sinbad.

Sinbad the Sailor is an imaginary seafarer and the protagonist of stories that originated in the Middle East. Sinbad is portrayed as a rich merchant living in Basra (a city that still exists in modern day Iraq), during the Abbasid era. The stories are of the seven voyages that he undertook because of his quest for adventure. All the voyages are fantastical in nature. During his voyages through the oceans he has bizarre escapades going to mystic places, encountering giants, monsters, and weird wonders.

The same kinds of adventures are there in many cultures, from Homer's Odyssey to tales in Indian mythology. All of them have one thing in common: curiosity that leads to exploration and fantastical experience.

When Einstein was asked about intelligent children he is purported to have said, ""If you want your children to be intelligent, read them fairy tales. If you want them to be more intelligent, read them more fairy tales." The fairy tales convey curiosity and adventure, children are awe stricken and spellbound. These stories amplify curiosity and intrigue children to explore and build their own fantasies, fantasies that could develop interest, curiosity and motivation.

It is true that when we become adults and travel to other countries, we begin to appreciate that we share more things in common with people in those countries. At the same time, we also take note of differences in attitudes between them and us. My own experience is illustrative of this fact. I had never travelled beyond my own country until I finished medical school. Even within India, I had rarely travelled outside my region. My worldly outlook came from reading books and magazines. My first forays were to Thailand, Malaysia, and the Philippines in South East Asia. I was in my early 20's and each place was unique yet similar. The people were different in how they behaved and led their lives but yet it had the same common features. It was an eye-opener. The sights, smells, and sounds were brand new experiences.

This led to my interest to experience life in many other countries. I lived in Barbados in the West Indies, and then went to Butner, a small town in North Carolina with just a few thousand people who know one another, and then to Singapore. In Barbados, a small island with about a quarter million people, life was intimate, people knew each other and soon I got to know many of them and began to experience their way of life, time was slow and less hectic but still tasks were completed and work was done. My experience in each of these places left an impact that I carried with me to my next home. This learning based on experience shaped me as it shapes all of us and helps us live in this world.

The learning we all want is more than learning from books. This is not the learning that schools and educational systems emphasize but it the learning that drives and builds us as individuals who are curious innovators. In addition to the experiential learning that derives from our external world, there is so much that we can do within our personal care, habits, and routines to positively influence our ability to learn.

The Art of Learning

Nutrition and its impact on learning and education have been of great interest and attention. From the time we are young, we have been advised to start our day with breakfast and eat balanced food. Intuitively it makes sense. I cannot think of any mom that does not fret when her child does not get up and eat breakfast. Everyone assumes eating breakfast is key to a healthy life; and that it gives a good start to the day and maybe makes kids smarter. But what is the data when it comes to breakfast?

The brain, the base of learning devours most of the energy (sugar/glucose), almost a fifth of our entire energy consumption. Energy consumption in youngsters' brains increases from birth until 4 years of age and is almost twice that of the adults relative to their size. This degree of energy consumption in children stays at this extraordinary level until 9–10 years of age. It then progressively drops to adult levels by late adolescence. The brain during these early years is quickly growing and changing as it helps the child adapt to the world by learning and using knowledge. It is a very critical time in development. Therefore, it seems logical that constant energy supply by a balanced diet is very important in children. Indeed malnutrition and poor diet during this susceptible period can lead to permanent consequences.

Children are very susceptible to changes in diet but not as much as we think. A multitude of micronutrient deficiencies can disturb the brain growth and by inference affect learning and therefore education. These deficits include minerals like iron, zinc and vitamin B12 folate. In most industrialized economies these micronutrient deficiencies are rare except in unusual conditions. The link between extremely poor nutrition and poor brain growth and mental development is clear in children, but it rarely happens under normal conditions.

So it is not surprising that numerous studies show that breakfast improves brain development and cognition in malnourished children. Free breakfast packages in schools, particularly in emerging and poorly developed countries and inner cities, have become common as a way to improve nutrition and thus improve learning and education.

Do these programs work?

Three studies showed enhancements in mathematics in Jamaican schoolchildren; in total pooled scores of language, reading, and math in US low-income students; and in vocabulary scores in Peruvian children. In all these studies, partaking in the school breakfast program meaningfully increased school attendance and could have been one of the reasons for improvement in learning. At least, providing breakfast at school improves school attendance and improves learning. They do not necessarily prove that eating breakfast improved learning.

Obviously, breakfast improves thinking and learning in children either directly or by increasing attendance. The remaining question is whether breakfast helps learning and cognition in well-nourished children. Studies have shown that undernourished children did better after breakfast than after a prolonged fast, but that this was not the situation for the well-nourished. In the studies in Jamaica and Peru, only the malnourished children significantly diverged in performance between the fed and the fasted states.

In a small study of children who habitually eat breakfast, skipping breakfast even once significantly reduced their professed level of energy and cheerfulness, but it did not affect their intellectual performance throughout the morning.

Putting it altogether the data imply that skipping breakfast interferes with cognition and learning, in malnourished children but not so in well-nourished children. For those of you who do not have a breakfast every morning (number is more than 50%) there is no need to feel guilty or think that you will have difficulty during the day. But if you habitually eat breakfast skipping breakfast can make you cranky and ill tempered.

In concept, the kind of breakfast one eats ought to affect brain growth and cognition. But a cooked meal compared with a cereal-and-toast breakfast, or breakfasts with different fat and carbohydrate composition, did not affect cognition or learning. The energy capacity of the breakfast meal may play a role. One study noted that a breakfast that provides 25% of the daily energy needs enhanced performance on a creativity test in a study of ten-year-old children compared with a breakfast that had less than 10% of energy needs. In the US more than 80% of children eat breakfast because of school programs, with almost at third having breakfast at school. In Singapore a small 2002 study found that almost a third of a group of teenage boys did not have proper breakfast in the morning on a regular basis.

Today, in many countries, the problem is overeating and overconsumption of calories leading to rapidly rising rates of obesity. The overconsumption happens everywhere at work, at home and at school. One of the biggest causes is the easy accessibility and enticement to consume soft drinks, which are heavily overloaded with sugar and snacks with extraordinary calorie content. Reducing easy accessibility of these temptations is one way to decrease weight gain and obesity. This is part of a drive to forbid soft drink vending machines in schools in the US.

To sum it up, breakfast is indeed good for the child but if a child skips breakfast and is otherwise healthy and well-nourished then there is nothing to worry about. Equally true for us adults. But regulating the overall nutritional content, reducing calorie intake and increasing physical activity will lead to better health and at lead to improved learning at school.

The Art of Learning

Let's not Forget Sleep

When we sleep we are not aware of what is happening around us. Many theories and questions exist about why we sleep, but no definite clear-cut answers to the questions. The truth is, we have no idea why we sleep. One intriguing possibility is that we need to sleep to consolidate memories.

During sleep we are not storing new material into the brain. Rather sleep transforms new and primarily labile memories coded in the conscious state into more fixed and constant representations integrated into the grid of previous long-term memories. Matched with a wake interval of equal length, a period of sleep boosts retention of newly learnt material and improves performance in various performance skills. Even small bursts of sleep as short as 6 minutes help this process; but sleep that is longer strengthens memory better.
Sleep supports the consolidation of memory of all types, but especially those that are consciously encoded, such as when we learn new material and even more so when it is behaviourally relevant to the individual.

So how does this happen?

Memory, as we discussed earlier, involves many parts of the brain. When a memory is encoded there is both a temporary storage, such as when we try to note down a set of instructions, and a longer storage of information. Memory formation is conceptualized as a route in which neuronal activity in specific brain circuits stimulates lasting synaptic changes. The consolidation process is seen as the re-activation of neuronal circuits that were involved in the initial encoding of the information. In rats, the patterns of neuronal firing that occur in the brain during simple tasks are re-activated in the same order during subsequent sleep.

In humans, there is similar data showing memory consolidation after sleep. So when we are awake and learning, memory is coded in both the temporary store and the long-term store; and during sleep there is repeated re-activation of the memories newly set in the temporary store, and that drives parallel re-activation of corresponding sites in the long-term store. This process stimulates the integration of the fresh memories in the network of long-term memories.

So what does this mean for learning? How do we use sleep to promote learning?

First, it means that the old adage, "Have a good night's sleep before an exam," has validity. College students memorized pairs of unrelated words. Half were then encouraged to take a nap and the other half stayed awake. During a retest, napping heightened the performance of those who initially did well on the test, but not on those who did poorly on the initial test exactly as predicted. Even very short naps improved learning.

In high school and college, sacrificing sleep to study especially just before exams is very common and many are chronically sleep deprived. In fact more than 60% get insufficient sleep (< 8 hours per night). Presumably, when students trade sleep for studying, they do so in the belief that the increased studying will help their grades.

In a study that asked whether reducing sleep, as students are prone to do, affects learning, researchers asked high school students to keep a diary of how long they studied and how long they slept, and then how they did on tests and quizzes the following day. They found that poor performance was related to reduced sleep. If teenagers do need to study more than usual, they should not sacrifice sleep to do it, but rather some other time-wasting activity. If they still need to spend time awake then they should get a nap before school or class or exam.

The Art of Learning

Baker's Dozen: A Few Tips to Help Students Learn

Goals, Motivation, and Feedback

In sum, motivation is linked to desire, expectation that one can meet the desires, and by self-confidence. The more uncertain we are that our own actions can lead to the desired outcome, the less confidence and motivation we have to undertake and persist with the task. This perception of being in charge of our own fate is very important. At a young age, the confidence is very fragile even though there maybe interest and motivation. The motivation could be extrinsic, meaning the student wants to do well and please their parents or teacher; and it may also be intrinsic because they are curious and eager to learn. Losing the momentum is very easy at this early age.

When students first start to learn a subject, they differ in their desire, expectations of achieving that desire, ability and confidence. Initial confidence comes from prior experience, attitude and ability. Students who are confident in their ability to learn have the ability to learn and are in an environment where their success can be attributed to their work; where they can develop motivation to learn and succeed. If nurturing is not right then the student is likely to lose motivation and interest.

When students attribute success to ability and hard work, it reinforces confidence and increases motivation to learn. It also builds a sense of who they are and how capable they are. It builds a sense of self-worth and self-esteem that in turn influences self-confidence and motivation. To enhance motivation, clear achievable and measurable goals must be at the foundation. Then measuring and judging the progress and making adjustments become the engine for maintaining interest and motivation.

The Art of Learning

Positive Feedback

Give positive but realistic feedback. Give positive feedback on level of competence, such as praise for the work done or actual measurable change in performance. This increases self-directed motivation, whereas negative performance feedback or criticism diminishes it. When we want to try something new we often find friends and family cheering us on. Go to any soccer game for children and you will see parents yelling, "You can do it!" This can help a person to try and get started but is not enough by itself to build confidence unless the person does well when they are performing the task.

Tell children to expect feedback. It is important for them to know and expect realistic feedback on what they do and to understand that it is not on them as a person. The timing is also important. Feedback should be given as close to the event or task as possible. If you give feedback a day, a week or a month later, the impact is much smaller and harder for the child to reconnect.

Motivation is enhanced when students perceive they are making progress in learning. In turn, as students work on tasks and become more skilful, they maintain a sense of self-confidence for performing well. Sometime how we provide feedback can enhance confidence. Confidence gets boosted when students are told they did just as well or better than others especially when they see someone else fail. This increased confidence leads to more perseverance in continuing to try the task.

Feedback is also very important in building confidence. Feedback should be immediate and specific. When someone is starting new endeavour, praise for early success helps improve confidence and increase motivation. Praising effort boosts confidence and motivation, but feedback that says you need to work harder reduces both.

The Art of Learning

Similarly letting people know they are good at the task increases confidence. This feedback works in the short term, but we do not know how well it works in the long term.

Confidence is a key to developing and maintaining motivation. Psychologists use the term *self-efficacy* to describe what in essence self-confidence is. Self-efficacy is the judgement by the individual on their ability and capacity to undertake a task. Confidence relates to how much effort is needed. Interestingly when students watch television as a vehicle for learning they report much less effort and more confidence then when they have to read material. But the learning was not any greater in other word more confidence and less effort does not translate into more learning.

1. Promote Independence

This feedback and competence must go with a sense of independence to result in increased self-directed motivation. This sense of independence, and therefore internal control, is extremely important in fostering motivation. Choice and the prospect for self-direction boost motivation by stimulating independence. Classroom studies in schools show that teachers who encourage autonomous thinking compared to controlling teachers catalyse greater inquisitiveness, self-directed behaviour and motivation. So, as a parent, you are better off praising performance, autonomous thinking and self-direction. Children of parents who support independent thinking do better in terms of creativity, inventiveness, resilience and curiosity than children of parents who are controlling or micro managing. In the long-term when the independent self-directed behaviour and motivation is integrated and assimilated with the personal development of the individual, it becomes intrinsic and self-directed. The greater we manage to internalize our interest and desire for what we are doing, it becomes part of our nature and the extrinsically motivated actions now become self-determined and intrinsic.

2. Do Not Use Fear or Punishment

It is probably even worse if the behaviour is solely shaped by fear of punishment. When that fear disappears the motivation also vanishes.

Students who are unduly controlled by outside factors rewards and punishments lose originality and learn less well to think on their own, especially when learning is complex or requires abstract, resourceful thinking.

3. Watch Others Perform and Succeed

The second most important influence on confidence to perform is by observing others perform the same task. If we see a friend or someone else that we think or estimate is similar to us in capability performing the task then we think we can do it. When children see other children try a task and succeed they are more likely to feel confident and try. This works better in motivating than watching a teacher solve the problem. Seeing many children perform well is better than seeing just one other person doing well in motivating the child to try. However just seeing others undertake the task and succeed is less convincing than one's own performance. Let's say we see a friend succeed in learning how to swing the golf club and then we try, if we are able to pick it up quickly then we end up feeling that we can indeed learn how to play golf. But if we have difficulty our confidence can get sapped and we could give up.

4. Set Goals

At this young age it is hard for children to build goals and work towards them. Guiding them in building and sustaining goals is a gentle art. Too much and you turn them off, too little and they do not learn how to set and reach goals skills that are important as they get older.

From these factors students derive cues signalling how well they are learning, which they use to assess efficacy for further learning. Show them that a little bit of nervousness before they start a task is completely normal. A little bit of "butterflies' is good but too much and it hinders our performance.

5. Avoid the Illusion of Knowing

Most young children cannot properly judge what they do and don't know. They also normally overestimate how well they comprehend the material when they are finished studying. This "illusion of knowing" is mirrored in the assertion that many children make after they obtain a poor grade on a test: "I studied so hard. I knew the material cold. I am shocked I failed."

Luckily, a mounting body of work has recognized how to improve their ability to judge what they do and do not know after studying. Recent research provides techniques that you can use to help children overcome this illusion of knowing so that they can spend their time studying material that they do not know so well.

The cue-only delayed judgment of learning procedure. This is a mouthful but a simple way to help your children know their comprehension of their material better.

Step 1: Test how much they know of the subject. Test after a delay. A longer delay may be better, but even an hour is good. With young children make it fun. Give them confidence praise their effort and performance do not just talk about what they do not know.

Step 2: Ask them to tell you what they remember. Then fill in what they forgot or misunderstood. Use clues and cues to help them remember, the more you make it like play the better the interaction. If you want to test using cues do not have the answers on the same page.

Step 3: Ask them how well they will do a test on that question. They will be able to judge quite well but they will not usually link it to what they need to focus on. Young children (3rd graders and

The Art of Learning

below) have difficulty extending their judgement in choosing what to study, while older children (fifth graders and above) can choose better by focusing on what they do not know.

Step 4: Help them turn the judgement and maybe help them focus on what they do not know. This is deliberate practice.

Step 5: Repeat the sequence.

This makes the learning time more productive and focused.

This technique has three critical features: test the material later after a significant delay (an hour, a day); two, when testing whether they know the concepts or not, check first with recall and only later with cues and make sure the answers are not visible and three, teach children to judge how likely they are to get the correct answer on a test. All three are critical and work well in total. This works whether they are learning vocabulary, a foreign language, or science or a reading passage.

Suppose you are helping a child study for the PSLE exam and there are essential points that the children are expected to learn and understand. Schedule a review session for some days after the child studied the topic at school and maybe completed their homework. And better after they worked on material other than the one that you want to see if they know the subject.

Ask 10 or so key questions that are the essential concepts of the material. Then ask them to answer the question and gauge if they think whether or not they know the answer for each question.

After making these judgments, tell the children to review the material and find out the answers for every question that they had trouble with.

This procedure should be used repeatedly.

Now let's talk about tests and exams. I know you know and we know that these assessments leave a lot to be desired, but we need to get through them in order to move ahead. How do we help our children overcome these obstacles?

6. Practice, Practice, Practice

No matter how confident your child may be, unless he or she practices over an extended period of time they will not be optimally primed or ready.

When should you start teaching the child how to study? Start as early as you can the sooner the better. Get them to learn that cramming is not a good way to learn.

The day you know the date when they will be taking the test, or in Singapore the Primary School learning Examination (PSLE), you can begin working with them to set goals and schedule a plan to study. What do you practice on? Test materials and format that is as close as possible to the real test or examination. Find as many practice tests as you can, the more the better.

Know your child; know their strengths and more important weak points. After they take their first practice test, take a close look, what were they good at, what did they have trouble in and what was easy. Then rank order the subject areas, starting with that they know cold and ending with what they know very little of.

So the rank order might look like this:

1.   Vocabulary
2.   Algebra
3.   Geometry
4.   Trigonometry
5.   Reading a passage
6.   Writing

9. Set their goals and structure learning based on this review

This review of your-self becomes the structure for your deliberate practice. In other words, practice with them more of what they know less and less of what they know more.

Keep testing and adjusting based on their performance. Bearing in mind the simple (almost too simple) mantra: poorer the performance more the practice.

Now obviously if they do not know the topic at all, or if it feels like an alien language, just repeating the test will not be beneficial. So you need to find a way to teach the topic so that it may be understood. You can learn by reading material, watching YouTube videos on the subject, ask a teacher to explain or better still a helpful friend who is good in that subject. Then use that to help them learn.

If it is math, find sample problems with solutions and then try having the child solve similar problems. Intersperse learning from sample problems to actually solving problems. If you can, look and test them with problems that use similar principles but are more varied and not exactly the same. This makes them think and learn when to use what approach to solve problems.

10. Space learning sessions

How do you space learning sessions? Remember Ebbinghaus, the longer he waited the more he forgot and the longer it took for him to relearn. In the case of tests and examinations you want the child to be ready at the time of the exam. You are less worried about how well they will do a year later or ten years later. All you want is for them to do well before the test or exam, so keeping the forgetting curve in mind you should have them take the last practice test before the exam as close to the exam date as possible before the exam.

The Art of Learning

Whenever you start, let's say your objective is for them to score 90% on the test or final exam; then when you do the diagnostic test you know their strengths and weaknesses and you can build a schedule to reach and maintain that criterion level. For weak areas it may take more sessions to reach that level and for strong areas it might take fewer sessions.

Obviously the more test sessions the better, but one way to think about arranging your sessions is to retest before you forget. Two interesting studies illustrate this very well. In the first of these studies, pupils studied Swahili–English word pairs. The interval between study sessions extended from 5 minutes to 14 days, and they were then tested 10 days after the first session. The length of time between sessions had a very large effect on test scores, with the 1-day interval yielding the best recall. In a second experiment, students learned the names of obscure objects. They used a 6-month RI, and the interval between sessions varied from 5 minutes to 6 months and the students were tested 6 months after the initial session. The optimal interval was 1 month. The optimal time between sessions (spacing) is directly related to how long you have to remember that is how long before you take the test.

The shorter the time before taking the test, the shorter the time needed between study sessions. From a study of 1300 subjects the optimal time between study sessions ranges from 10-30% of the time before the test.

So we would suggest studying more difficult and harder topics in more number of sessions; that is maybe at 10% interval and the easier in 30% interval. This incorporates both the principle of deliberate practice and spacing. Let's take an example: say your child has a PSLE exam in 10 weeks; his weakest section is vocabulary and strongest geometry. Then you would space their learning so that they study vocabulary every week and geometry every 3 weeks. This will give them more time and effort for the weak subject; deliberate practice yet enough spacing, and less time for doing well on the stronger subject, with more spacing and continued retention of knowledge.

11. Mix it up

Unless they are just studying one topic (and even if they are) try to mix things up. Over learning the same thing is tedious and, as we have discussed, it is not the most effective method of learning.

So if you can mix up subjects during learning: a session on algebra, followed by vocabulary and then geometry or the other way about. If they are working on a topic, mix worked out problems with practice problems and work on problems from more than one topic. This will be what they will have to do on a test anyway, so why not practice that way? The more they practice as though they are taking the real test, the better the learning will be. They will know the skill but also, equally important, when to use what skill where and when.

This is just like getting ready for a game be it tennis or cycling. You have to mix skills, training on one element of the game with other elements. And most importantly you have to practice playing the whole game. Each skill by itself will not be enough and taking each piece of the test without taking the whole test or examination will not optimize readiness.

12. Learn with friends

Learning towards a target like a final examination can seem like a solitary effort but it need not be. Working with friends, sharing knowledge, teaching each other can make this journey more rewarding. You may want to form a peer group with likeminded parents that can meet once in a while to talk about places to find more practice tests and discuss approaches to topics that you find difficult.

13. Use tests or practice as close to what you will be tested on

In any topic, there are usually many resources that you can find. But the ones that you want to use should be those that give your child more practice for whatever test or examination that they are studying towards. So more than just watching and reading, practicing more will make the difference. This is not to say that they do not need to first understand the basics of whatever they are learning but to say that is not enough. If they do not know the basics they will be better served by watching and learning from the web, asking peers (or, even better, someone who just took the exam and did well), asking teachers and faculty, or heaven forbid going to the library and reading a book. No matters how, knowing the basics are fundamental to success; imagine playing tennis if you do not know how to hold a racquet.

The Art of Learning

7 Rules of Learning for SAT, and other Tests

If you are student at some point or another you will have to take examinations and tests that determine your fate or at least it seems that way.

The following apply to how you should prepare for examinations.

The First rule

Practice, practice, practice,

—and not just the day before the test. Even if you are very confident, if you do not practice over an extended period of time you will not be optimally primed or ready. When should you start? The day you know the date when you will be taking the test. If you know when then you can set goals and schedule a plan to study. What do you practice on? Test materials and format that is as close as possible to the real test or examination. If you are taking the SAT, ACT, LSAT, MCAT or anyone of the three four letter abbreviations or something else, find as many practice tests as you can, the more the better.

The Second rule

Know yourself; know your strengths and more important weak points. After you take your first practice test, take a close look, what were you good at, what did you have trouble in and what was Greek or Latin to you. (I assume you do not know either language well). Once you do that rank order the subject areas starting with that you know cold and ending with what you know very little. So the rank order might look like this:

1. Vocabulary
2. Algebra

3. Geometry
4. Trigonometry
5. Reading a passage
6. Writing

The Third rule

Set your goals and structure your learning based on this review. This review of your-self becomes the structure for your deliberate practice. In other words, you practice more of what you know less and less of what you know more.

You will spend more time with writing then vocabulary and less algebra then trigonometry. I wish I could tell you how much time you should spend on each or what percentage of your time should be allocated to each subject. But that will be a guess and a very crude one I am afraid. Better for you to keep testing yourself and adjusting your schedule based on your performance. Keeping in mind the simple, almost too simple mantra: poorer the performance more the practice. Now obviously if you do not know the topic at all or if it feels like an alien language just repeating the test will not be benefit. So you need to find a way to learn the topic. You can learn by reading material, watching YouTube videos on the subject, ask a teacher to explain or better still a helpful friend who is good in that subject. In other words if your understanding of the topic is very limited learn it a bit more before you get back into the repeated testing mode. If it is math find sample problems with solutions and then try your hand on solving similar problems. Intersperse learning from sample problems to actually solving problems. If you can, look and test yourself with problems that use similar principles but are more varied and not exactly the same. This makes you think when to use what approach to solve problems.

Remember Ebbinghaus, the longer he waited the more he forgot and the longer it took for him to relearn. How do you space your learning sessions? In the case of tests and examinations you want to be ready at the time of your exam. You are less worried about how well you will do a year later or ten years later. All you want is to do well before the test or exam, so keeping the forgetting curve in mind you should take your last test before the exam as close to the exam date as possible before the exam.

Whenever you start let's say your objective is to have 90% on the test or final exam, and then when you do your diagnostic test you know your strength and weakness and you can build a schedule to reach and maintain that criterion level. For your weak areas it may take you more sessions to reach that level and for your strong areas it might take you fewer sessions.

Obviously, the more your test sessions the better, but one way to think about arranging your sessions is to retest before you forget. Two interesting studies give you an idea. In the first of these studies, pupils studied Swahili–

English word pairs. The interval between study sessions extended from 5 minutes to 14 days, and they were then tested 10 days after the first session. The length of time between sessions had a very large effect on test scores, with the 1-day interval yielding the best recall. In a second experiment students learned the names of obscure objects, they used a 6-month retention interval, and the interval between sessions varied from 5 minutes to 6 months and they were tested 6 months after the initial session. The optimal interval was 1 month.

The optimal time between sessions (spacing) is directly related to how long you have to remember that is how long before you take the test. If you have only a short time until your test, then you should shorten the time between study sessions. From a study of 1300 subjects the optimal time between study sessions ranges from 10-30% of the time before the test.

So I would suggest that you study your more difficult and harder topics over more sessions that is at 10% interval, and the easier, at 30% interval. This incorporates both the principle of deliberate practice and spacing. Let's take an example you have a SAT exam in 10 weeks, your weakest section is vocabulary and your strongest geometry. Then, you would space such that you study vocabulary every week and geometry every 3 weeks. This gives more time and effort for your weak subject - deliberate practice but yet enough spacing and less time for your stronger subject but more spacing and continued retention of knowledge.

The Fifth rule

Unless you are just studying one topic and even if you are try to mix things up. Over learning the same thing is tedious and from what we have discussed not the most effective method of learning.

So if you can, mix up your subjects by scheduling, say, a session on algebra followed by vocabulary and then geometry. If you are working on a topic mix worked out problems with practice problems and work on problems from more than one topic. This will be what you will have to do on a test any way so why not practice that way. More you practice like taking the real test the better your learning. You will know the skill but equally important when to use what skill where and when.

This is just like getting ready for a game be it tennis or cycling. You have to mix skills training on one element of the game with other elements and most important you have to practice playing the whole game. Each skill by itself will not be enough and taking each piece of the test without taking the whole test or examination will not optimize your readiness.

The Art of Learning

Learning towards a target like a final examination or SAT can seem like a solitary effort but it need not be.

Working with friends, sharing knowledge, teaching each other can make this journey more rewarding. Today with all the different social communication tools you can engage with and become part of a learning network that is neither geographically or time zone constrained. You may want to form a peer group that can meet once in a while to talk about places to find more practice tests, discuss approaches to topics that you find difficult and maybe help others, remember teaching others enhances your own learning.

The Seventh rule

In whatever topic you are studying usually there are many resources that you can find. But the ones that you want to use should be those that give you more practice for whatever test or examination that you are studying towards. So more than just watching and reading, practicing more will make the difference. This is not to say that you do not need to first understand the basics of whatever you are learning but to say that is not enough. If you do not know the basics you will be better served by watching and learning from the web, asking peers or even better someone who just took the exam and did well, asking teachers and faculty, or heaven forbid going to the library and reading a book. No matters how, knowing the basics are fundamental to success; imagine playing tennis if you do not know how to hold a racquet.

The Art of Learning

Resources to Consider when Studying

Khan Academy
https://www.khanacademy.org/youcanlearnanything

With more than 16 million users this is the giant space for learning. Its impact has been enormous for school children, college students and literally the millions of people who log onto the site to learn. Let's say you want to prepare for some of the common entrance examinations this is a good place to start. It shows the structure of the exam, the common problems and worked out solutions and then this serves as a base for practice tests. Learning particular subjects is built based on many of the principles that we talked about and it helps monitor progress.

Bozeman Science
http://www.bozemanscience.com/about/

Where is Bozeman? Bozeman is a city in Montana, United States in the south western part of the state with a population of just over 37000 people. Out of this small town has emerged an outstanding site for students to learn science.

Bozeman science is the brainchild of Paul Andersen who has been teaching high school science at the local high school. He started teaching science on YouTube and that has evolved into this outstanding program that is engaging and very clear in helping you understand science. The program although mostly directed to Advanced Placement examinations in the US is very relevant to learning science for all. What is particularly noteworthy is that it makes students think about how to solve problems Paul is at present a science teacher and at Bozeman High School.

Testpreview.com
http://www.testpreview.com/

These are places to look for practice tests. Besides the usual places such as the sites of the developers of the examination new sites that

provide   additional   practice   tests   is   4sites.com   and
Testpreview.com. The sites give access to a number of tests from
graduate entry exams Graduate Exams:
• GMAT
• GRE General
• LSAT
• MCAT

To High school exams and college entrance tests, High School
Exams
• ACT (American College Testing Program.)
• AP Biology
• AP Chemistry
• AP US History
• SAT subject tests
• SAT Scholastic aptitude test

The Art of Learning

8 Tips for Raising Children

What can we say about learning and children? Parents always want the best for their children. Just type "learning for babies" into Google search and you will get more than 70 million web hits. There is even a Baby TV web site for babies and toddlers.

From even before the baby is born and all the way to kindergarten play groups to chat rooms, Facebook the one conversation that immediately evokes interest; how to raise a smart, intelligent baby. Parents feel guilty that maybe they should have been listening to Mozart when the baby was in the womb or their child will grow up being dumb.

If you go to preschool and hear the parents talk, they worry about making sure they get their child everything, to move ahead, get into the best college or university. That anxiety means a tremendous sale of many popular videos to make your child a "Baby Einstein" and giving tiny toddlers, iPads. Do they really work? Most of the studies show they do not. In fact they may actually slow word learning. It may be because placing an iPad in front of a baby keeps them occupied but that is not the same as interacting with the baby, Good "outmoded" one-on-one parent-to-baby contact. It just does not seem cool. It may be the circumstance that for every minute a baby is in front of a screen, they are not interacting with a caring, parent ... and babies learn from loving parents more than words they learn to engage and build emotions.

Talking to your baby, playing with your toddler, giving attention to what interests your child and use that to nurture curiosity builds the connections that stimulates and helps the child grow and develop. So let's start with some simple nuggets—pearls not rules, I do not want to use the word rules in case you take it so seriously that if you do not follow them you will be hurting your child. Children are resilient and I think they will grow up fine as long as you give them lots of love, a bit of stimulation and allow them to be curious and explore.

The Art of Learning

#1 Give attention and love

It sounds corny and cliché but of all things that you can do this is the most important. Lack of love and attention can damage your baby. This is true not just for humans but also for animals. In 1922, Hammett showed that rarely handled rats were more timid, fearful than rats that had been stroked and handled.[27] If you isolate rat pups they do not grow and their brains develop poorly. Just a little bit of stroking restores both their growth and brain development.

Sensory touch is important for even the development of worms. Worms that are isolated grow up smaller and their brains and connections in the brain are less well formed. Just tapping the plate on which the worms were growing a few times restored the development of the worm.[28]Human babies are the same; they need nurture and touch. Orphaned infants in the old days did not receive touch and attention and this was linked to poor growth and brain development.

Preterm infants are usually kept in incubators, isolated from their parents and caregivers. In a very elegant little study, 20 preterm neonates were touched for 15 minutes three times per day for 10 days. The infants were stroked gently for the first and final 5 minutes, and their limbs were gently bent upward during the middle 5 minutes. The stimulated infants when compared with un-stimulated infants of the same gestational age (approximately 31 weeks), birth weight and duration of intensive care. The infants who were touched were bigger almost 47 % greater weight and spent more time awake and active.[29]

---

[27](Hammett FS. Studies of the thyroid apparatus: V. The significance of the comparative mortality rates of parathyroidectomized wild Norway rats and excitable and non-excitable albino rats. Endocrinology. 1922;6:221–9)
[28] (Rose JK, Sangha S, Rai S, Norman KR, Rankin CH. Decreased sensory stimulation reduces behavioral responding, retards development and alters neuronal connectivity in Caenorhabditis elegans. J Neurosci. 2005;25:7159–68)
[29] (Scafidi F, Field T, Schanberg SM, et al. Effects of tactile/kinesthetic stimulation and sleep/wake behavior of preterm neonates. Infant Behav Dev. 1986;9:91–105.)

The Art of Learning

A toddler's brain changes swiftly during the first years of life, especially the first three years. It is a time of rapid mental, language, social, emotive growth. For example the child begins to learn to understand sounds, connect sounds to objects, form words and build language around 15–18 months. Rapid language learning carries on into the preschool years and becomes the base for further growth.

The youngster's brain develops as she or he hears sees, tastes, smells and feels. Every time the child uses a sense to perceive the world, a neural connection is made each new experiences echoed many times help grow the brain and strengthens connections, which form the way the child learns, thinks, and behaves.

A close and loving relationship between the child and the parent is the best way to nurture the child's growing brain. When a parent plays with a child and sings, smiles, gestures, speaks points out, or tells a story to the child the total experience leads to the child's growth and development. All that you have to do is see a mother and I would say father and their interaction with 2-month-old infant and you see the way in which the bond develops. Babies need lots of care and affection in the early years. Cuddling, babbling and talking to the child are better than giving them an IPad with lots of games. The human touch beats an IPad any day.

#2 Let Children Play by Themselves and With Others

Toys are amusing, but toys are also tools that aid children learn about themselves and the realm around them. When you see puppies or kittens what you see is their playful nature, they get into everything and they learn by exploring. Babies, toddlers love to play, explore and get into things. Yes they put things into their mouth and put their finger where they shouldn't but that is how they learn. This natural curiosity should be given as much room as possible but with safety in mind. Play is essential to the healthy growth of children.

As children play, they learn to develop the fine and gross motor skills, to get along with others and to grow. Play helps a child do the following:

• Develop physical and motor skills

Gross motor skills develop along with the natural evolution of the child and as a child learns to sit, crawl, run, climb, reach, grasp and climb. Fine motor skills are advanced as children handle small objects, cups, and spoons.

• Develop language skills

In the earlier section on reading and language we discussed the role of what they hear as the key to developing first recognition and then expression of words and hence language development.

Language grows as a child plays and relates with others. This begins with parents playing, cooing and babbling games with their children.

• Develop social skills

Learning to collaborate, taking turns and playing by the rules are essential skills learned in early play and interaction with other children. Learning to share becomes an integral element of growth and social skill development. These skills mature as the child plays.

• Develop concepts

Children, by playing, touching and moving, start to build an idea of their surroundings and their role in the space around them. They learn to solve problems (What does this do?) through play. Previously we discussed about number sense and math development, this comes into shape as the child begins to notice and count objects in their space. Children also learn colours, size and shapes. Children move on to higher levels of thought as they play and interact with games and objects both physical and online in a more stimulating environment.

Parents are children's first and paramount playmates. Children become more creative when their parents or other children are involved in their play. When the parent truly plays with the child rather than just providing the toys or supervising this leads to the social and creative growth of the child.

Becoming part of a child's play is natural for some but awkward for other parents. It will take practice. Some ideas for how to play with your child include:

- First Observe. Watch your child carefully to learn what he or she can do and what they have trouble performing. See what they like and enjoy.
- Then Follow. Join in and play with your child with what they enjoy doing. Be it peek a boo or hiding things or tapping their toes, touching their face so that the child knows you are interested in what he or she is doing. Let your youngster be in control and control the course of play. This holds true whether the child is an infant or an adolescent, knowing their interest and interacting with them becomes the basis of long term sustained relationship and personal growth.
- Third let your creative and playful juices flow. Use toys and daily objects in diverse ways, and you will be astounded at how many ways you can play with one object.

Choosing a toy
- First is the toy suitable for the child's age, skills and capabilities?
- Will it keep the child's interest?
- Is it safe? Are there any would-be dangers such as sharp edges? Can it be swallowed?
- Does it provide practice in fine and or gross motor skills?

Toys from Birth to 1 year old

A baby absorbs and soaks everything from their surroundings by using all five senses (touch, sight, smell, hearing, taste,). So they will put things in their mouth or stick them into their noses. Avoid toys that are too small, sharp or pointed.

Toys for this age group include:
- Plastic mirrors
- Rattles
- Picture books
- Musical toys
- Squeeze toys
- Teething toys

As a child gets older
- Puzzles
- Mechanical toys
- Books to read
- Real and interactive games. (Note: Xbox PlayStation or Nintendo may become more appropriate but the key at any age is not to give gifts of playthings as a substitute for interaction. The objects and toys are not substitutes; they are add-ons. They are unlikely by themselves to enhance growth and development.)

#4 Watch what you do around children. They learn from what you do, not what you say

Children imitate. So if you tell them do not lie and then they see you doing just that, guess what they learn to do what you do.
The well-known psychoanalyst Carl Jung says it succinctly: "If there is anything that we wish to change in the child, we should first examine it and see whether it is not something that could better be changed in ourselves."

#5 Answer questions that children come up with even if it appears silly

How many times have you faced this situation?

The facial expression is a classic: intense focus, furrowed brows, eyes wide open and a question that leaves you speechless, the room, eerily quiet and silent. Children wouldn't be children if they didn't habitually let loose the sort of question that gives everyday parents an awkward moment. These questions are explorations that address the types of subjects that have confounded parents from time immemorial.

What to do when your child asks:

Where did I come from?

How was I born, did I come out of Moms stomach?

Who is God?

How do you know he exists?

Who was there before God?

What happens after we die?

The thing not to do is to say: "keep quiet" or "I will tell you later" or "Go ask your Dad"

The answer depends on the age and the question. Learning why the child is asking the question and what he thinks is the answer then lets you frame an appropriate answer to the question. But avoiding the question means it tells the child not to ask or that it is a bad question. It does not give you a chance to see where they are coming from. Look at it as an opening to chat and a chance to help clarify and in many cases reduce an unstated fear.

#6 As children get older, ask them questions that will get them to think

When children are very young, asking questions about something they see or hear gets them to think and answer. Promoting curiosity could be by playing games, say make different sounds and ask the child to guess the answer. Or show pictures and ask what they are or could be used for. This becomes a two-way street, the child soon explores by asking questions of you and others it induces their natural curiosity to flourish and grow.

The manner in which you ask the questions matters. If you give your child the chance to answer with one word (yes, no), then you will get a one-word reply. Therefore try to ask open-ended questions to allow the child to think and answer and keep an exchange going.

When your child goes to school? Better to ask what they did at school and what was the best experience that day rather than asking, "Did you have a good day?" Framing the questions with a positive angle is better than questions that have a negative focus. Getting children to read and understand will help them, as they get older, to infer what comes next. This type of questioning is important especially when learning concepts. Asking them questions like "what happens if," is a good way to make them think about potential consequences of various actions.

Conceptual understanding builds by this kind of exploration and questioning. Equally important is the principle of elaboration. Asking them to explain why and how they answered a question helps increase retention and connects the new knowledge to their existing framework of information. So when your child predicts something ask why, ask them to explain.

When they come up with a solution ask for alternatives. This tactic makes the child think could there be other options. It allows more creative thinking maybe helps by building bridges to what they already know. With older children asking them to search, look it up on the net and see what other possible alternative explanations are out there again opens up thinking and building their own paths to explore and think for themselves.
Discourse and discussion are the basis of intellectual development and creating curiosity so when you see or discuss use this as a

chance to explain what happens when they see something or draw to explain.

#7 Keep the child curious and creative

We all know that creativity can lead to the generation of novel and worthwhile solutions to a given problem or situation. It includes the generation of unique but appropriate content, as in the case of music and the arts.

Without creativity as the driver, there would be no progress and evolution of our lives on this planet. To fill the best jobs available in today's knowledge- and information-based societies, we would need people who are creative and equipped with innovative thinking.

Training can help develop more creativity, as more than 70 studies have shown, and there are specific strategies that help. Let me outline a few:

- The first and often underrated element is necessity. As the cliché goes, necessity is the mother of invention. This has implications for how to enhance creativity in childhood and school. Research suggests that posing difficult problems leads to enhanced creativity. So introducing tough problems for children to think keeps them inventive and curious. Maybe the solutions are impractical but still encourage them to put their thinking cap on.

- Another way to enhance creativity is to insert an element of absurdity when they are working on a question or problem. This is well illustrated in a small study with 20 college students who were required to read an absurd short story based on Franz Kafka's short story A Country Doctor. Afterward, the students were given a test. They were twice as accurate as and better on the test than another group of 20 students who had read a different but coherent story. So, we can assume that by their having read "unexpected absurdity" the first group's unconscious ability to access hidden patterns had been

218

enhanced. I think this will work with any age introduce absurdity and that makes you think differently. Read them Dr Seuss and see what they do and think.

- A third and well-recognised approach is to think of a problem by re-conceptualising it or looking at it from the opposite angle. Just looking at the problem from another angle leads to better and innovative solutions. This demonstrates that people can create higher-quality concepts when compelled to reconceive a problem in different ways before trying to solve it. Bringing opposing ideas together at the same time as the usual conventional thoughts leads to integrative ideas that are novel and valuable. In all these instances we are trying to keep the curiosity fire burning without quenching it. The questions to ask are "So what?" and "What if?" For children this is more natural than for adults, they often think from a different vantage point that adults, listen, encourage and discuss.

#8: Do not forget emotional growth

Most parents and even educational institutions, schools and colleges emphasise the thinking aspect, or cognition. Less attention is paid to the emotional aspects. Yet, emotions are important as they play a vital part in learning, and can help or hinder a child's academic commitment and success in school.

Positive emotions directly relate to interest and self-motivation, which drive the attitudes critical for acquiring knowledge; negative emotions like depression are linked to the converse. Positive emotions and motivation increase our attention at a task. We have all had instances where we were so involved in an activity we like, such as reading a book, playing a game or solving a difficult problem, time stands still and we become disconnected from the clamour of everyday life. Some aspects of emotional development could be genetic. Others are learnt in the context of the environment of the growing child.

But emotional development is not just genetic. In fact, the first five years of life present an irreplaceable prospect to lay the groundwork for healthy emotional and social development. Research has shown that negative early experiences impair this in children. Maternal attachment is important: The amount of quality time mothers spend with their children relates to the children's emotional development. There are many elements of emotional competence.

The first and an indispensable aspect is our willingness to hear what others have to say. In other words, we have to be good listeners. From one's early school days to one's professional life, this is an essential skill and a determinant of emotional quotient (EQ). For a child to develop this means watching and learning by imitation a parent listening to them and then in turn learning to listen. Teaching them this skill by being a role model is very important.

The second crucial component is our ability to perceive emotions in individuals. This plays a major role in modulating interactions and conversations. Children learn by watching how we react to them and then in turn they recognize our emotions.

The third and equally important point is to use this awareness of emotions in responding to people and events or what is said, in an appropriate manner. This may be in the context of participating in discussions in a polite manner, learning to assert or disagree, to reason, argue or persuade without getting personal. Again this develops by seeing others in action especially parents, teachers and other role models.

A natural consequence of these skills is the development and organisation of values, which include being sensitive towards others. Values are exemplified not by words, but by actions, such as ethical behaviour, respect for others, commitment and accepting responsibility. If you want to keep your child growing and ready for this world that we living in keep these nuggets in mind.

Afterword

We have come to the end of the book. I hope you enjoyed the book and that you will use some of what I have described in your journey into the world of learning.

As you prepare to set sail let me blow a little bit of breeze to move you onward and forward. I encourage you to go back and read sections that you have trouble recalling. Use the very principles in this book to learn what you need to help you as you move forward into an exciting exploration of learning.

Remember the key principles of learning as you take action. They are simple in theory but as most things in life needs to be executed to succeed.

First and foremost is the desire to learn and having goals that are clear and near in time will set the direction to sail. Knowing where you want to go helps organize and plan a path to navigate to reach that goal. Once you set sail, practice, practice, and practice more. Practice more of what you do not know and less of what you know. If you are learning by listening to a lecture or reading a book, recall what you just learnt and then check to see what you missed. If you need to remember for a longer time space the interval between learning sessions and if you can mix it with other material that you have to study. Connect what you learnt with what you already know the more you connect the better you remember.

Finally, explore be curious and learn by experience. Never lose the joy of curiosity. Have fun.

The Art of Learning

Reading List

Why we see what we do: redux
By Dale Purves and RB Lotto 2011
This is a wonderful and tightly knit book on how we perceive the world around us. Real-life instances, and plainly accessible arguments, the book can be easily read and understood by individuals with slight or no education in neuroscience, as well as more advanced readers. It has a companion web site (http://www.purveslab.net/main/) that one can enter and see for themselves the nature of vision and perception. The book clearly points out how perception is not what we see but how we interpret what we see.

Memory: A Contribution to Experimental Psychology:
Issue 3 of Columbia University Teachers College: Educational reprints. no. 3
By Hermann Ebbinghaus Edition reprint
This reprint from 1913 is the classic in the field. The translation from the original German is clear and captures the elegant thoughts of Ebbinghaus as he self-explored memory. The book makes for fascinating reading and one that is well worth the effort. The sheer magnitude and fastidiousness of the endeavour that Ebbinghaus undertook was staggering and immense. Just for an experiment on repetition he learnt and relearnt over 400 series of 16 syllables.
His description of how he interpreted the results of his self-experiments have stood the test of time.

Why We Do What We Do: Understanding Self-Motivation, 1996By Edward L. Deci, Richard Flaste
This book similar to Dale Purves book on perception challenges popular assumptions on what motivates us. Society today from schools to work use rewards to motivate. In this concise and persuasive book Deci argues otherwise. He shows that our assumption about rewards is erroneous. He argues it is better to

222

motivate by showing why a particular course path or task important and then permitting as much personal freedom to achieve stimulates interest and motivation than rewards do. The key is autonomy and intrinsic motivation.

Learning Theories: An Educational Perspective (6th Edition) Unabridged, By Dale H. Schunk
Dale H. Schunk is Dean of the School of Education and Professor of Curriculum and Instruction at the University of North Carolina at Greensboro.
A useful resource provides an understanding of the main principles, ideas and research in learning as they relate to education. The book is aimed more for teachers and educationists. It is a bit dense to read but for those who spend the time and energy it provides a valuable insight into the science of learning as it relates to how we educate students.

Talent is Overrated: What Really Separates World-Class Performers from Everybody Else,2010 By Geoffrey Colvin
This book has two main points' first practice, practice, practice and second practice deliberately. Practice especially deliberate practice is indeed very effective if we can motivate ourselves to follow up. The title may make the point a bit more forcefully than the data. Other factors do matter in every endeavour but effort and practice are nominally under our control and something that we could influence by our own actions. The others our genes and our environment are not under our control.

Thinking, Fast and Slow Paperback – April 2, 2013 By Daniel Kahneman, Farrar, Straus and Giroux; Reprint edition, 2013
This is a best seller from Nobel Laureate who in clear and precise terms introduces the concept of two modes of thinking fast and slow. These modes of thinking and the decisions that stem from it drive choice and behaviour.

Mindset: The New Psychology of Success, 2007
By Carol Dweck
Dweck a psychologist from Stanford confronts the mind-set problem. In organizations and in our own encounters we talk about mind-set as something that is relatively fixed or rigid. Here Dweck points out that yes mind-set could be fixed but if it is not and it can change and grow then the growth mind-set could be the spring for success. A fixed mind-set makes you set your sense of self as something that is difficult to change, you are who you are, and your destiny is to go through life evading challenge and therefore failure. A growth mind-set, on the other hand, is one in which you see yourself as capable of change and therefore success. Dweck offers a method to assess you or may be others and illustrates how a certain mind-set can affect many parts of life, from work to home.

Drive: The Surprising Truth About What Motivates Us, 2011
By Daniel H. Pink
In many ways this is an extension and addition to Edward Deci's book. This is a very readable and illuminating exposition of the role of motivation in modern life. He extends and connects the importance of intrinsic motivation to many aspects of our modern life. The book provides direct and practical advice on developing motivation.

The Learning Brain: Memory and Brain Development in Children, 2012
By Torkel Klingberg
The book complements the chapter introducing learning and memory. Here the author uses our understanding how the brain works to learning. The book emphasis is on "working memory"-- our capacity to focus and to keep pertinent data in our head while disregarding interferences. He discusses methods to improve and enhance working memory and how that can improve math and reading skills.

The Art of Learning

The Number Sense: How the Mind Creates Mathematics, Revised and Updated Edition 2011
By Stanislas Dehaene

This is a beautifully written book on how our mind creates math written by a mathematician neuroscientist. The book uses almost no jargon as it describes how we get our sense of numbers. Dehaene starts with the startling and novel introduction to the notion that animals--including rats, pigeons, and primates--can complete simple mathematical calculations, and that human infants also have a elementary number sense. Dehaene proposes that this rudimentary number sense is as simple to the way the brain comprehends the world as our perception of colour or objects, and, like these other capacities, our number sense is wired into our brain.

Reading in the Brain: The Science and Evolution of a Human Invention, 2009
By Stanislas Dehaene

This is the companion book to number sense. Here Dehaene introduces us to how we read. In this spellbinding exploration, Stanislas Dehaene delivers an accessible explanation of the brain circuitry of reading. Dehaene contends that the mind is not an empty slate: Reading and Writing systems across all cultures depend on similar brain circuits, and reading is only possible insofar as it fits within the limits of a primate brain. Reading is an example of neuronal reusing—the enrolment and use of formerly evolved neural circuits that were utilized for other purposes. Dehaene is one of the most talented writer of science; he makes the mechanisms of the mind less enigmatic, but no less incredible.

Self-Esteem: A Proven Program of Cognitive Techniques for Assessing, Improving, and Maintaining Your Self-Esteem, 2000
By Matthew McKay, Patrick Fanning

Interested in boosting self-esteem? Then this is an easy to read and practical guide. This is a very complete self-help book about the nature, basis und management of low self-esteem. It contains many exercises and suggestions some more practical than others for helping improve self-esteem and thereby boost confidence and motivation.

How to Develop Self-Confidence And Influence People By Public Speaking Mass Market, 1991By Dale Carnegie
The classic book by the well know father figure in this genre. The author, Dale Carnegie popularized building self-confidence and learning public speaking. Dale Carnegie wrote a clear and succinct book on public speaking that remains timeless and enduring. The book is very easy to read comprehensible, with many "practical" illustrations, and with a terrific summary at the end of each chapter.

Research-Based Strategies to Ignite Student Learning: Insights from a Neurologist and Classroom Teacher, 2007
By Judy Willis.
The spark that is needed to ignite a student's interest and motivate learning.
Dr Willis is a neurologist and a middle school teacher an unusual combination that allows her to use her neurology background to utilize and interpret research to foster interest and learning. The book is intended towards teachers but indeed can be useful for anyone interested in motivation and learning.

The Tyranny of Testing, 2003
By Banesh Hoffman Dover Publications (August 15, 2003)
This is a book that takes a hard look at standardized testing and its pitfalls. The book is worth a critical read and its evocative insights should give pause to anyone who uses standardized testing. Testing should be a tool for learning and not just a tool for assessing performance.

The Art of Learning

Begin Here: The Forgotten Conditions of Teaching and Learning 1991 By Jacques Barzun
A book that remains timely for its insightful critique of current systems of education and learning.

The Art of Learning

Suggested references

The following are excellent references:.

Perception
Why We See What We Do Redux: A Wholly Empirical Theory of Vision Dale Purves, R. Beau Lotto Sinauer Associates, Inc.; Second edition (November 5, 2010)

If you have the time and inclination you can enter this fascinating world by visiting
http://www.purveslab.net/main/

Ventriloquism
 Sum by WH, Polack I (1954) Visual contribution to speech intelligibility in noise. J Acoust Soc Am 26:212–215

Shams L, Kamitani Y, Shimojo S (2000) Illusions. What you see is what you hear. Nature 408:788

Mc Gurk H, Macdonald J (1976) Hearing lips and seeing voices. Nature 264:746–748
Christoph Kayser Æ Nikos K. Logothetis Do early sensory cortices integrate cross-modal information? Brain Struct Funct (2007) 212:121–132

Learning and Memory
 Anderson, J. R. (2000). *Learning and memory: An integrated approach* (2nd ed.). New York, NY, US: John Wiley & Sons, Inc.
 This is a great on the cognitive psychology of learning and memory:
Bransford, Brown, & Cocking. (2000). *How People Learn*. Washington, D.C.: National Academies Press.
Another terrific introduction to this topic:
Dunlosky, J., Rawson, K.A., Marsh, E.J., Nathan, M.J., & Willingham, D.T. (2013a). Improving students' learning with effective learning techniques: Promising directions from cognitive and educational psychology. Psychological Science in the Public Interest, 14(1), 4-58. This review is a classic. It examines and systematically looks ta what learning techniques work and what do not.

Dunlosky, J., Rawson, K.A., Marsh, E.J., Nathan, M.J., & Willingham, D.T. (2013b). What works, what doesn't. Scientific American Mind, September-October 2013.

This is a shorter (and easier to digest) version of the previous paper: Ebbinghaus, H. (1885). *Memory: A contribution to experimental psychology.* New York: Dover. This is the original classic work which frames much of what we know about learning even now.

Hebb DO; *The Organization of Behaviour.* 1949. John Wiley & Sons New York.

This is a classic book and has been a mainstay and basic foundation for understanding behaviour:

Del Giudice, M., Manera, V., & Keysers, C. (2009). Programmed to learn? The ontogeny of mirror neurons. Dev Sci, 12(2), 350-363. *This paper introduces the fascinating idea of neurons that are programmed to learn literally functioning as mirrors. A mirror neuron is active both when an animal performs and when the animal perceives the same act accomplished by another animal. The neuron "mirrors" the behaviour of the other, as though the viewer was itself performing.*

Pashler, H., Bain, P., Bottge, B., Graesser, A., Koedinger, K., McDaniel, M., & Metcalfe, J. (2007). Organizing instruction and study to improve student learning (NCER 2007-20204). Washington, D.C.: National Center for Education Research, Institute of Education Sciences, U.S. Department of Education.

Language learning

Dehaene S: *Reading in the brain.* New York: Penguin, 2009. Great review and introduction to this topic.
Dehaene S, Cohen L, Sigman M, Vinckier F. (2005 Trends Cogn Sci.). *he neural code for written words: a proposal.* **9** (7). pp. 335–341
Joseph, L. M. (2002). Helping children link sound to print: Phonics procedures for small-group or whole- class settings. Intervention in School and Clinic, 37, 217- 221.

Bear, D. R., Invernizzi, M., Templeton, S. R., & Johnston, F. (2003). Words their way: Word study for phonics, vocabulary, and spelling instruction. Upper Saddle River, NJ: Prentice Hall

Number sense

S. Dehaene: The number sense. New York: Oxford University Press, 1997; Cambridge (UK): Penguin press, 1997
Brian Butterworth, Dorian Yeo DYSCALCULIA GUIDANCE: Helping Pupils with Specific Learning Difficulties in Maths [Paperback] Nfer Nelson Publishing (1 Jun 2004)

Curiosity:
If you want to read one article that gives you an illustrative introduction to curiosity then this is the one:
Harlow, Harry F. Mice, monkeys, men, and motives: Psychological Review, Vol 60(1), Jan 1953, 23-32.
Berlyne, D. E.; Slater, J: Perceptual curiosity, exploratory behaviour, and maze learning.
Journal of Comparative and Physiological Psychology, Vol 50(3), Jun 1957, 228-232
This article is an interesting introduction to curiosity:
Berlyne, D.E. (1960). *Conflict, Arousal, and Curiosity.* New York, McGraw-Hill Book Company
Daniel E. Berlyne. Curiosity and learning: Motivation and Emotion June 1978, Volume 2, Issue 2, pp 97-175
This is the classic study of rats and their curiosity. Obstruction is by electrical grid:
Nissen , H. W. (1930). A study of exploratory behavior in the white rat by means of the obstruction method. J. Genet. Psychol., 1930, 37, 361-376

Motivation:
If you want to read just one piece then this is for you:
Hulleman, C.S., & Harackiewicz, J.M. (2009). Promoting interest and performance in high school science classes. *Science*, **326**, 1410-1412.
Other readings on motivation:
Harackiewicz, J.M., Rozek, C.S., Hulleman, C.S., & Hyde, J.S. (2012). Helping parents to motivate adolescents in mathematics and science:

An experimental test of a utility-value intervention. Psychological Science, 40, 899-906.

Harackiewicz, J.M., & Hulleman, c.S. (2010). The importance of interest: The role of achievement void and task values in promoting the development of interest. Social & Personality Psychology Compass, 4(1), 42-52.

Hidi, S., & Harackiewicz, J.M. (2000). Motivating the academically unmotivated: A critical issue for the 21st century. *Review of Educational Research*, **70**, 151-179.

If you want to just read one:

Lepper, M. R., & Greene, D. (Eds.). (1978). *The Hidden Costs of Reward. New Perspectives on the Psychology of Human Motivation.* Hillsdale, N.J.: Erlbaum.

Other readings on reward and motivation:

Lepper, M. R. (1983). Extrinsic reward and intrinsic motivation: Implications for the classroom. In J. M. Levine M. C. Wang (Eds.), Teacher and student perceptions: Implications for learning (pp. 281-317). Hillsdale, NJ: Lawrence Erlbaum Associates, Inc.

Bower, & N. H. Frijda (Eds.), Cognitive perspectives on emotion and motivation (pp. 37-61). Dordrecht, the Netherlands: Kluwer Sansone, C., & Harackiewicz, J. M. (Eds.). (2000). *Intrinsic and extrinsic motivation: The search for optimal motivation and performance.* San Diego: Academic Press.

Atkinson, J. W. (1957). Motivational determinants of risk-taking behavior. Psychological Review, 64, 359-372.

Mindset

Dweck, C. S. (1986). Motivational processes affecting learning. American Psychologist, 41, 1040-1048.

The Art of Learning

Dweck, C. S., & Leggett, E. L. (1988). A social-cognitive approach to motivation and personality. Psychological Review, 95, 256-273.

Confidence:
The article that gives you an overall perspective on confidence:
Bandura, A. (1977). Self-efficacy: Toward a unifying theory of behavioral change. Psychological Review, 84, 191-215.

Other articles on confidence and motivation:
The articles provide an introduction to Bandura's perspective on how learning and behaviour change happens and the importance of confidence.
They also illustrate the importance of confidence in building and sustaining motivation:
Bandura, A. (1989a). Human agency in social cognitive theory. American Psychologist, 44, 1175-1184.
Bandura, A. (1989b). Social cognitive theory. In R. Vasta (Ed.), Annals of child development (Vol. 6, pp. 1-60).
Marsh, H. W., & Shavelson, R. (1985). Self-concept: Its multifaceted, hierarchical structure. Educational Psychologist, 20, 107-123.
Schunk, D. H. (1989a). Self-efficacy and achievement behaviours. Educational Psychology Review, 1, 173-208.
Schunk, D. H. (1989b). Self-efficacy and cognitive skill learning. In C. Ames & R. Ames (Eds.), Research on motivation in education: Vol. 3. Goals and cognitions (pp. 13-44). San Diego: Academic. Bandura, A. (1986). Social foundations of thought and action: A social cognitive theory. Englewood Cliffs, NJ: Prentice-Hall.
Woolfolk, A. E., & Hoy, W. K. (1990). Prospective teachers' sense of efficacy and beliefs about control. Journal of Educational Psychology, 82, 81-91.

ABCD of Motivation:
This article examines the data on confidence and ability:
Zimmerman, B. Martinez-Pons, M. (1990). Student differences in self-regulated learning: Relating grade, sex, and giftedness to self-efficacy and strategy use. Journal of Educational Psychology, 82, 51-59.
Zimmerman, B. J., Ringle, J. (1981). Effects of model persistence and statements of confidence on children's self-efficacy and problem solving. Journal of Educational Psychology, 73, 485-493.

The Art of Learning

Illusion of knowing

Glenberg AM, Wilkinson AC, Epstein W: The illusion of knowing: Failure in the self-assessment of comprehension; Memory & Cognition 1982, Vol. 10(6), 597-602
Introduction to concept of illusion of knowing
Markman, E. M. (1977). Realizing that you don't understand: A preliminary investigation. Child Development, 48, 986–992.
Markman, E. M. (1979). Realizing that you don't understand: Elementary school children's awareness of inconsistencies. Child Development, 50, 643–655.
Nelson, T. O. (1984). A comparison of current measures of the accuracy of feeling-of-knowing predictions. Psychological Bulletin, 95, 109–133.
Perner, J. (1991). Understanding the representational mind. Cambridge, MA: MIT Press.
Pressley, M., Levin, J. R., Ghatala, E. S., & Ahmad, M. (1987). Test monitoring in young grade school children. Journal of Experimental Child Psychology, 43, 96–111.
Stipek, D. (1984). Young children's performance expectations: Logical analysis or wishful thinking?
Taylor, M., Esbensen, B. M., & Bennett, R. T. (1994). Children's understanding of knowledge acquisition: The tendency for children to report that they have always known what they have just learned. Child Development, 65, 1581–1604.
Wilson, R. A., & Keil, F. C. (1998). The shadows and shallows of explanation. Minds & Machines, 8, 137–145
G. Nicholls (Ed.), Advances in motivation and achievement, Vol. 3: The development of achievement motivation (pp. 35–56). Greenwich, CT: JAI Press.
These articles give the background and description of how we develop the illusion of knowing and how to overcome this

Marshmallow test

Mischel, W; Ebbesen, Ebbe B.; Rask off Zeiss, Antonette (1972). "Cognitive and attentional mechanisms in delay of gratification.". *Journal of Personality and Social Psychology* **21** (2): 204–218. The classic paper on delayed gratification.
Schlam, Nicole L.; Wilson; Shoda, ; Mischel, W; Ayduk, Ozlem (2013). "Preschoolers' delay of gratification predicts their body mass 30 years later". *The Journal of Pediatrics* **162**: 90–93.

The Art of Learning

:

Dweck, C. S. (2012). Mindset: How You Can Fulfil Your Potential. Constable & Robinson Limited.
Dweck, C. S. (2006). Mindset: The new psychology of success. New York: Random House.
These two books on mindset are a great introduction to Dweck's thinking and evidence supporting her concept:

Self -discipline

Duckworth, A., & Seligman, M. (2005). Self-discipline outdoes IQ in predicting academic performance of adolescents. *Psychological Science, 16* (12), 939–944.
The title of this book speaks for itself:

Self-regulation

Bandura, Albert (1997). Self-Efficacy: The Exercise of Control. Worth Publishers; 1st edition (February 15, 1997)
This book is a tour-de force by the pioneer on self-efficacy research. He summarizes this body of research in an easy to comprehend format. The work applies not just to learning but also in dealing with change and growth during our life. He explores this notion in amazing detail but still keeps it clear and digestible.
Schunk DH, Zimmerman BJ: Self-regulation and learning; In Handbook of Psychology Eds Reynolds WMi, Miller GE Wiley and Sons 2003 page 59-78
Schunk, D. H. (1982). Effects of effort attributional feedback on children's perceived self-efficacy and achievement. Journal of Educational Psychology, 74, 548-556.
Schunk, D. H. (1983a). Ability versus effort attributional feedback: Differential effects on self-efficacy and achievement. Journal of Educational Psychology, 75, 848-856.
Schunk, D. H. (1983b). Developing children's self-efficacy and skills: The roles of social comparative information and goal setting. Contemporary Educational Psychology, 8, 76-86.
Schunk, D. H. (1983c). Goal difficulty and attainment information: Effects on children's achievement behaviors. Human Learning, 2, 107-117.

Schunk, D. H. (1983). Reward contingencies and the development of children's skills and self-efficacy. Journal of Educational Psychology, 75, 511-518.

Schunk, D. H. (1984). Enhancing self-efficacy and achievement through rewards and goals: Motivational and informational effects. Journal of Educational Research, 78, 29-34.

Schunk, D. H. (1985). Participation in goal setting: Effects on self-efficacy and skills of learning disabled children. Journal of Special Education, 19, 307-317.

Schunk, D. H. (1987). Peer models and children's behavioral change. Review of Educational Research, 57,149-174.

Schunk, D. H. & Gunn, T. P. (1985). Modeled importance of task strategies and achievement beliefs: Effects on self-efficacy and skill development. Journal of Early Adolescence, 5, 247-258.

Schunk, D. H., & Hanson, A. R. (1985). Peer models: Influence on children's self-efficacy and achievement. Journal of Educational Psychology, 77,313-322.

Schunk, D. H., & Hanson, A. R. (1989). Self-modeling and children's cognitive skill learning. Journal of Educational Psychology, 81, 155-163.

Schunk, D. H., Hanson, A. R., & Cox, P. D. (1987). Peer-model attributes and children's achievement behaviors. Journal of Educational Psychology, 79, 54-61.

Thinking mechanism

Daniel Kahneman Thinking, Fast and Slow Paperback – April 2, 2013 Farrar, Straus and Giroux; Reprint edition (April 2, 2013)

This is a best seller from Nobel Laureate who in clear and precise terms introduces the concept of two modes of thinking fast and slow. These modes of thinking and the decisions that stem from it drive choice and behaviour. The pathway that is desirable for this purpose is the slow deliberative pathway

If-Then method

Sonuga-Barke, E. J. S. (2002). Psychological heterogenity in ADHD—A dual pathway model of behavior and cognition. Behavioral Brain Research, 130, 29–36.

Sonuga-Barke, E. J. S., Sergeant, J. A., Nigg, J., & Willcutt, E. (2008). Executive dysfunction and delay aversion in ADHD: Nosological and diagnostic implications. Child and Adolescent, Psychiatric Clinics of North America, 17, 367–384.

Sonuga-Barke, E. J. S., Taylor, E., Sembi, S., & Smith, J. (1992).Hyperactivity and delay aversion—I. The effect of delay on choice. Journal of Child Psychology and Psychiatry, 33, 387–398

Practice:

K. Anders Ericsson, Ralf Th. Krampe, and Clemens Tesch-Romer. *The Role of Deliberate Practice in the Acquisition of Expert Performance.* Psychological Review 1993, Vol. 100. No. 3, 363-406
This is the reference that has been made famous by Malcolm Gladwell in his book.
Guillermo Campitelli & Fernand Gobet (2011), *Deliberate practice: Necessary but not sufficient. Current Directions in Psychological Science*, 20, 280-285.
This is an article that points out the limits of deliberate practice.

Testing as learning

Bangert-Drowns, R.L., Kulik, J.A., & Kulik, C.L.C. (1991). Effects of frequent classroom testing. Journal of Educational Research, 85, 89–99.
Bjork, R.A. (1975). Retrieval as a memory modifier: An interpretation of negative recency and related phenomena. In R.L. Solso (Ed.), Information processing and cognition: The Loyola symposium (pp. 123–144). Hillsdale, NJ: Erlbaum
Jeffrey D. Karpicke, Roediger H: The Critical Importance of Retrieval for Learning
Science 319, 966 (2008)
Henry L. Roediger III and Jeffrey D. Karpicke; The Power of Testing Memory: Basic Research and Implications for Educational Practice
Perspectives on Psychological Science 2006 1: 181

The Art of Learning

Art of Memory

Yates, Frances A. (1966). *The Art of Memory*. Chicago: University of Chicago Press
This is the book that gives a broad perspective on systems of improving memory.

Borella, E., Carretti, B., Riboldi, F., & De Beni, R. (2010). "Working memory training in older adults: Evidence of transfer and maintenance effects". *Psychology and Aging* 25: 767–778.
Klingberg, T., Forssberg, H., & Westerberg, H. (2002). "Training of Working Memory in Children with ADHD". *Journal of Clinical and Experimental Neuropsychology* 24 (6): 781–791.
Harry Lorayne and Jerry Lucas; The Memory Book: The Classic Guide to Improving Your Memory at Work, at School, and at Play Ballantine Books; Reissue edition (Aug 27, 1996)

Imagery

Lesgold, A. M., McCormick, C., & Golinkoff, R. M. (1975). Imagery Training and children's prose learning. Journal of Educational Psychology, 67(5), 663–667.
Anderson, R. C., & Kulhavy, R. W. (1972). Imagery and prose learning. Journal of Educational Psychology, 63, 242–243

Spaced learning

Cepeda, N. J., Coburn, N., Rohrer, D., Wixted, J. T., Mozer, M. C., & Pashler, H. (2009). Optimizing distributed practice: Theoretical analysis and practical implications. Experimental Psychology, 56, 236–246.
Cepeda, N. J., Pashler, H., Vul, E., Wixted, J. T., & Rohrer, D. (2006). Distributed practice in verbal recall tasks: A review and quantitative synthesis. Psychological Bulletin, 132, 354–380.
Cepeda, N. J., Vul, E., Rohrer, D., Wixted, J. T., & Pashler, H. (2008). Spacing effects in learning: A temporal ridgeline of optimal retention. Psychological Science, 19, 1095–1102
Landauer, T. K., & Bjork, R. A. (1978). Optimum rehearsal patterns and name learning. In M. Gruneberg, P. E. Morris, & R. N. Sykes (Eds.), Practical aspects of memory (pp. 625–632). London: Academic Press.
Rea, C. P., & Modigliani, V. (1985). The effect of expanded versus massed practice on the retention of multiplication facts and spelling lists. Human Learning, 4, 11–18.

The Art of Learning

Rothkopf, EZ; Bisbicos, E. SELECTIVE FACILITATIVE EFFECTS OF
INTERSPERSED QUESTIONS ON LEARNING FROM WRITTEN
MATERIALS. Journal of Educational Psychology, Vol 58(1), Feb 1967,
56-61

Spitzer, H. F. (1939). Studies in retention. Journal of Educational
Psychology, 30, 641–656.
Zechmeister, E. B., & Shaughnessy, J. J. (1980). When you know that
you know and when you think that you know but you don't. *Bulletin
of the Psychonomic Society, 15*(1), 41-44.

Mixing it up
Martina A. Rau1, Vincent Aleven1 and Nikol Rummel Blocked versus
Interleaved Practice with Multiple Representations in an Intelligent
Tutoring System for Fractions V. Aleven, J. Kay, and J. Mostow (Eds.):
ITS 2010, Part I, LNCS 6094, pp. 413–422, 2010. © Springer-Verlag
Berlin Heidelberg 2010
Kornell, N., & Bjork, R. A. (2008). Learning concepts and categories: Is
spacing the "enemy of induction" Psychological Science 19, 585-592)
Taylor, K., & Rohrer, D. (2010). The effect of interleaving practice.
Applied Cognitive Psychology, 24, 837–848).

MIE and Hole in the wall
Dr. Sugata Mitra, Dr. Ritu Dangwal, Shiffon Chatterjee, Dr. Swati Jha,
Ravinder S. Bisht and Preeti Kapur Acquisition of computing literacy
on shared public computers: Children and the 'Hole in the
Wall' *Australasian Journal of Educational Technology 2005, 21(3),
407-426.*
Parimala Inamdar and Arun Kulkarni
Hole-In-The-Wall' Computer Kiosks Foster Mathematics
Achievement - A comparative study *Educational Technology &
Society, 10 (2), 170-179 (2007)*
Mitra, S. & Dangwal, R.
Limits to self-organising systems of learning: the Kalikuppam
experiment
British Journal of Educational Technology, Vol 41 No 5 2010.
Ritu Dangwal and Preeti Kapur

The Art of Learning

Elaborative learning
Martin, Vicky L.; Pressley, Michael
Elaborative-interrogation effects depend on the nature of the question.
Journal of Educational Psychology, Vol 83(1), Mar 1991, 113-11

Ava Johnsey Gary R. Morrison, Steven M. Ross
Using elaboration strategies training in computer-based instruction to promote generative learning
Contemporary Educational Psychology, Volume 17, Issue 2, April 1992, Pages 125–135

Self-Explanation
Bielaczyc, K., Pirolli, P., & Brown, A. (1995). Training in self-explanation and self-regulation strategies: Investigating the effects of knowledge acquisition activities on problem solving. .*Cognition and Instruction, 13(2)*, 221–252

Concept learning
Feldman, Jacob (2003). "The Simplicity Principle in Human Concept Learning". *Psychology Science* 12: 227–232.
Merrill, M.D. & Tennyson, R.D. (1977). Concept Teaching: An Instructional Design Guide. Englewood Cliffs, NJ: Educational Technology

Summarization:
Bonnie B. Armbruster, Thomas H. Anderson, Joyce Ostertag Source: Reading Does Text Structure/Summarization Instruction Facilitate Learning from Expository Text? Author(s): Research Quarterly, Vol. 22, No. 3 (Summer, 1987), pp. 331-346

Experiential learning by living
Kolb. D. A. and Fry, R. (1975) 'Toward an applied theory of experiential learning;, in C. Cooper (ed.) *Theories of Group Process*, London: John Wiley.

240

Kolb, A. and Kolb D. A. (2001) *Experiential Learning Theory Bibliography 1971-2001*, Boston, Ma.: McBer and Co,

Clark, J., & White, G. (2010). "Experiential Learning: A Definitive Edge In The Job Market". *American Journal Of Business Education*, 3(2), 115-118.

The Art of Learning

186, 190, 192, 197, 200,
206, 207, 208, 209
Learning Curve, 29, 30
Link technique, 125
Massed learning, 36
memory, 3, 12, 17, 18, 21, 22,
23, 24, 25, 26, 27, 28, 29, 30,
32, 33, 34, 35, 36, 38, 42, 45,
85, 108, 109, 110, 115, 116,
117, 124, 125, 127, 130,
131, 132, 134, 135, 136,
141, 145, 147, 163, 170,
171, 176, 205, 207
Mind-Set, 5, 79
Mix It Up, 6, 86
Mnemonic, 124, 125
Motivation, 3, 5, 20, 31, 36, 49,
50, 51, 52, 53, 54, 55, 57, 58,
59, 60, 62, 63, 64, 69, 70, 71,
74, 75, 80, 81, 85, 86, 89, 91,
95, 96, 102, 106, 113, 150,
160, 165, 172, 179, 180,
181, 202, 206, 207, 208, 209
Negative feedback, 57
Novelty, 52, 53
Number sense, 4, 45
P2P U, 8, 152, 153
Peeragogy, 8, 152, 153
Perception, 17, 124
Phonemes, 42, 43, 44

Practice, 6, 7, 9, 86, 109, 110,
113, 142, 143, 146, 183,
204, 206
Practice retrieval, 7, 116
1
Recall, 4, 6, 23, 86, 116, 121,
134
Repetition, 32, 108, 109, 121,
123
Repetition, 7, 106, 111
Rewards, 5, 57, 60
Rheingold U, 8, 152
Right Spacing Interval, 8, 136
Rules, 3, 14, 27, 55, 85, 123,
195, 197
Self-control, 5, 73
Self-Discipline, 6, 103
Self-explanation, 9, 163
Self-Set Goals, 6, 90
Sleep, 9, 176
SOLE, 8, 151, 154
Space, 6, 9, 86, 184
Space your learning, 8, 130
Storage, 4, 23
Sum it up, 9, 167
Summarizing, 36, 167
Team LEAD, 12
Today, 13, 43, 148, 175, 190
Toys, 10, 197, 198

About the author:

Dr Krishnan started his career in psychiatry at Duke in 1981.

He identified the role of silent strokes in the development of depression and cognitive impairment. This work was funded by numerous grants and by a National Institute of Health Center grant. He received numerous awards for his research. Including Laughlin Award, American College of Psychiatry, 1984;Collegium Internationale Neuro-Psychopharmacologicum Rafaelsen Fellowship Award, 1988;Walker P. Inman Memorial Fund Grant for a study of extra-pituitary regulation of cortisol, 1984;Dorfman Award, Best Paper in Psychosomatics, 1990;NARSAD Distinguished Investigator Award for Genetic Imaging Study in Bipolar Disorder granted by National Alliance for Research on Schizophrenia and Depression (NARSAD) 1996-98; Honoured Teacher Award, Department of Psychiatry & Behavioural Sciences, Duke University Medical Centre, 2001; Gerald Klerman Award for Research in Mood Disorders, Depressive and Bipolar Support Alliance, 2002;Burlingame Award: Institute of Living 2008; AAGP Distinguished Scientist Award, 2007; Geriatric Psychiatry Award,: American College of Psychiatry 2009; Mood Disorders research award American College of Psychiatry 2015;Listed in Marquis 'Who's Who in Science and Engineering, since 1996.

He was also elected to the Institute of Medicine National Academy of Sciences USA.. He has published extensively with over 460 articles and numerous book chapters and books. He is recognized for pioneering research on neurological and cognitive basis of depression and the link between cardiac disease and depression. In 1998 he became Chair of the department of psychiatry at Duke. The department was large with over 400 faculty. In a short span of time he grew the research portfolio substantially placing the department amongst the top 5 departments of psychiatry for many years. As part of the educational effort they built an innovative and extensive continuing medical education network that featured satellite delivery of content, live lectures and archived web based material. This was at that time recognized as the leader in continuing psychiatric education.

The next phase of his career started when Duke signed an agreement in 2005 to build a new medical school in Singapore. He became Dean of Duke- NUS in 2008. His job was to start creating the school and develop the education and research infrastructure.

The school has developed and implemented a new and exciting method of learning called Team LEAD. This program has attracted global attention and is now used at many other institutions including duke in North Carolina and high schools in Singapore.

American Association of Medical Colleges (AAMC) published this approach as a case study. He and his faculty built a world class Academic Medical Centre in joint partnership with Singhealth. His experience in leading and building a 21st century educational institution with education based on science has led to his writing a series of commentaries for "Today" and form the basis for the present book.

www.ingramcontent.com/pod-product-compliance
Lightning Source LLC
LaVergne TN
LVHW022322080426
835508LV00041B/1692